HOW TO START A RIOT

HOW TO START
A RIOT

Support Your Local Jesus Revolution

JONATHAN STORMENT

LEAFWOOD
PUBLISHERS

HOW TO START A RIOT
Support Your Local Jesus Revolution

Copyright © 2014 by Jonathan Storment

ISBN 978-0-89112-604-1

Printed in the United States of America

Cover design by ThinkPen Design, Inc.
Interior text design by Sandy Armstrong, Strong Design

For information contact:
Abilene Christian University Press
1626 Campus Court
Abilene, Texas 79601

1-877-816-4455
www.leafwoodpublishers.com

14 15 16 17 18 19 / 6 5 4 3 2 1

To my best friend and wife Leslie.
You are a parable for me of the love of God.

To my parents, for teaching me how to love the LORD
and my mom for teaching me to love to read.

To Josh Graves, for your consistent encouragement to
just write something down and for your constant hope
in a Jesus who is making all things new.

To the good people of The Hills Church of Christ and
Highland Church of Christ, for allowing me to share these
dangerous ideas about the resurrection to a group
of people eager to put some skin on it.

And to Rick Atchley, for mentoring, loving, and supporting
my family. Thank you especially for your generosity with your
ideas. You gave me some of the most powerful ideas and
language to talk about the kingdom of God and then told me
not to quote you. You'll notice I honored your wishes.

Contents

Acknowledgments

It takes a village to raise a child; and it takes something like that to write a book. This book started off as a sermon series for a local church. Only by many readers, editors, and friendly suggestions has it been turned into what you are holding.

Special thanks to Leafwood Publishers for the helpful edits, to my friends David Ayers, Josh Graves, Sara Barton, Brian Shackmann, Luke Norsworthy, Jake Jacobson, Nell Sims, Lindsey Pierson, Wade Hodges, and Matthew Atchley for reading through this and making contributions.

Since this book has been in me for almost ten years, there are countless scholars and preachers and other writers and friends that have added to it. I've tried to remember and cite each time an idea came from somewhere else, but I'm sure I've missed a few. So consider this a hat tip "to the unknown scholar." I'm grateful to stand on your shoulders.

This book started for me in a ten-person Church of Christ that has long ago closed its doors but opened my heart for the Kingdom of God. I will always be grateful to the people who grew me up, and I hope that is reflected in these pages.

Since Churches of Christ gave me this story, I'd like to give it back to them. All of my profits from this book will go to "A Restoration Movement" (the vision of the Highland Church of Christ). So feel free to buy some extra copies for your friends and family!

Thanks for reading, and remember: "Support Your Local Revolution."

Jonathan Storment
January, 2014

How to Read This Book

This is a book about a book that turned the world upside down. It's a book about resurrection and community and a resurrected community. It's about women and men who were nothing but peasants and fisherman who somehow stood up against the principalities and powers of the world . . . and won.

It's about rulers and kings and Caesars who desperately want to maintain the status quo and will go to the most violent lengths to do so. And it's about how, with all their power and weaponry, they fail to get a single Jewish carpenter to stay dead.

It's a book about the book of Acts. Which is itself a book about all sorts of books.

That's the first thing you should know about Acts. Acts is a book that is in conversation with many other books of Scripture. It's written by a first-century Jesus follower named Luke who is trying to tell the story of Jesus; and he's telling this story *in a certain way*. Because Acts is the second part of the story Luke is telling. His first book is creatively titled in your Bible "Luke," and it's about the gospel of Jesus. His second book, Acts, is about what the community that Jesus gathered does with that gospel.

The second thing you should know when reading this book is that Acts doesn't stay in one time or place. Luke is constantly making allusions to other stories in the Scriptures. He quotes Isaiah more than any other New Testament writer, he talks about and refers to Abraham dozens of times, and he is constantly alluding to the book of Genesis.

All of these are intentional winks Luke is making at us, the readers of this Jesus story. He wants us to know that this story is bigger than a few decades and a handful of people in some remote country in Palestine. It's about God entering and reclaiming his entire world.

This is a book about a God who is still doing that.

Despite what you may have seen or heard about Christians and churches, this is who God wants his people to be. Not, as Martin Luther King Jr. once warned against, "bastions of the status quo," but a group of people who catch the wind of the Spirit and allow it to carry them wherever it may blow.

If you are opening the book of Acts for the first time, you may be surprised to see how often the simple telling of the story of Jesus stirs up all manner of protests and disorder in city after city. Whenever a community of faith catches this vision of God alive and at work in his world, it can still start a riot.

Prologue

On a pleasant spring evening in Paris, May 1913, a riot broke out because of a ballet. It was titled mildly enough, "The Rite of Spring"; but after a few minutes in, the composer broke all of the conventionally accepted rules for staging a ballet. And within a few more minutes, the room exploded.

People were booing and screaming; elderly people hit each other with their canes. And the composer ran out in tears.

You know, just like the last time you went to the ballet.

Michael Gungor writes about this riot in his book *The Crowd, the Critic, and the Muse,* and points out that this happened back in a time when people weren't accosted by the constant noise of advertisements and Spielberg explosions. This happened back when people actually listened to the music and allowed themselves to be immersed in the experience.

This happened back when people used to pay enough attention to what was happening to riot.

To be honest, I hesitated to write this book. If you are paying close attention to the culture we live in, this book can seem to strike the wrong chord. It seems we already know how to start riots. Our conversations have become more and more shrill, and our culture wars have become entrenched, and it seems everybody is angry.

But as I point out in this book, our problem is not passion, it is *the things that we are passionate about, and the way we are passionate about them.*

I'm writing this book from the Bible Belt of the U.S. and if you are reading it somewhere else, there is a chance that the language of riots is more than just a metaphor for you, so let me hurry to add that I'm not trying to promote anarchy.

This isn't a book about starting another political shouting match, or another Twitter religion war. And it certainly isn't trying to get Christians to become violent. It's a book trying to wake Jesus followers up to the implications of following Jesus.

One of my concerns about writing this book is that we will see the bloody knuckles of Jesus and forget that the blood on his knuckles belongs to Jesus. One of my concerns is that, in re-visiting what Rodney Stark calls "The Triumph of Christianity," we might forget that Jesus and Christianity triumphed in a very different kind of way. The way of self-giving sacrifice.

I wrote this book because somewhere in the past hundred years, the idea of the resurrection of Jesus has begun to be seen as a "conservative" idea, something that enforces the way things are. But for most of Christian history it has been the exact opposite.

I wrote this book because there is something breathtaking about the first Jesus followers. They are risky and gentle, kind and convicted, imprisoned and compassionate, dying and yet fully alive. I wrote this book because I have always wanted to get in on that.

And I suspect I'm not the only one.

Chapter 1

Support Your
Local Revolution

"On the whole I do not find Christians outside of the catacombs sufficiently sensible of conditions. Does anyone have the foggiest idea what sort of power we so blithely invoke? Or as I suspect does no one believe a word of it? The churches are children playing on the floor with their chemistry sets, making up a batch of TNT to kill a Sunday morning. It is madness to wear ladies' hats and straw hats and velvet hats to church; we should all be wearing crash helmets. Ushers should issue life preservers and signal flares; they should lash us to our pews. For the sleeping god may wake someday and take offense, or the waking god may draw us out to where we can never return."

> —Annie Dillard[1]

"I don't know what's going to happen, but I know I'm going to jail."

> —Martin Luther King Jr., leaving a Good Friday service in Birmingham, Alabama[2]

Back when I was a junior in college and my wife, Leslie, and I were just dating, we were driving down the Interstate and the speed limit seemed a bit restrictive. Since plenty of people were going well above the posted limit, I got behind a line of cars that was going right beneath Warp 9. Surely, I thought, if a cop was going to pull anybody over, he would get the cars that were leading the pack. Not the innocent rear car that was just trying to keep the pace.

What police officer could crack that genius code?

We found one. He came out of nowhere and pulled behind us, lights and sirens blazing. Then, as we pulled over, he made some hand gesture waving us off and went on to pursue the cars ahead. So we sat there, left to stew in our guilt, as he pulled over the equally guilty minivan in front of us.

After a minute or two passed, Leslie wondered out loud why we were sitting there. "You know he wasn't pulling you over."

"Babe, I'm pretty sure he was," I replied. "He did that whole hand gesture thing as he went by us."

"No," she said, "he was just waving, thanking us for letting him by." That made a lot of sense.

Wow, I began to think. How stupid we must look, sitting here on the shoulder of the Interstate. Slowly I pulled back onto the highway, putting on my blinker like any good law-abiding citizen would. As we drove by the police officer, we returned his polite hand gesture.

Apparently the highway patrolman *was* pulling us over. Immediately, he ran back to his car and punched the accelerator. Just a few seconds down the highway, he flew past us. And that's when it dawned on me—"he thinks we are running from him." So we pulled over again.

Now in front of us, the policeman yanked his car onto the shoulder. He had to back up almost a third of a mile. Sliding to a stop right in front of our bumper, he jumped out of his car and ran over to our van (have I mentioned we were driving a minivan). He yanked me out of the van while he screamed at me. Before I realized what was happening, he began to frisk me.

Have you ever been frisked? If you haven't, don't judge me. Something about being patted down brings out a primal response in a guy. Immediately, I had my own personal Genesis 3 kind of moment. I wanted to blurt out, "This woman that was given me, she's why I was speeding."

The whole experience actually turned out okay. More than okay. When the police officer realized what had happened, he couldn't stop laughing. We actually took a picture with him, and he wound up giving us one of those Jr. Texas Deputy stickers for us to wear. Obviously we are pretty hardcore. But I'll never forget that experience. It was the closest I have ever come to being in serious trouble with the law.

One of the things that might surprise you if you are picking up the Bible for the first time is how often the earliest Christians were in trouble with the law. They were in jail more than the 1980s Dallas Cowboys.

Now, I'm not recommending that lawbreaking should be a characteristic for which we are known. I'm not suggesting that we modern Christians should try to match the time spent in jail by those first followers of Jesus. But I find there is something inspiring about this. A lot of these men and women are peasants. Many of them are slaves. They're at the bottom of society. They are nobodies.

And they are going to change the world.

That's really what you see in the book of Acts. Acts is this revolutionary manifesto of common people turning the world upside down.

I grew up hearing that the main purpose of Acts was to give us correct doctrine on whatever the burning issues of the day happened to be. I grew up with the idea that the book of Acts was about learning how to do church right. It was some kind of blueprint for modern churches. If they did it, we were supposed to. If they didn't do it, woe to any of us if we did do it. I'm very grateful for the churches that raised me, and the tradition that taught me to love the Lord and Scripture; but somehow, we never did recommend that we

Christians today ought to go to prison or get beaten or stir up riots as often as those believers in Acts. Nobody seemed eager to imitate *that part of Luke's record of the early church.*

Theologian N. T. Wright says Acts could be accurately named "Another Day, Another Riot." I think that raises the question, "So how did Christianity go from that . . . to what it is today?"

If you ask most people—at least Western people—what they think about Christianity, they probably will give you a pretty domesticated vision of church. Church is a place known for weddings and funerals, a place where the woman who sells you Mary Kay spends her Sunday mornings.

After all, when was the last time you saw crowd control at a church?

Study after study keeps rolling out, telling us that a growing number of Americans think religion is at best irrelevant and obsolete. That the Christian faith is filled with people who are hypocritical and exclusive and mean. Church is generally becoming seen, not as a compelling force for good, but as a way of making the world *a worse place.*[3]

My background is in Churches of Christ, and one of the reasons I love my heritage is that we traditionally have tried to get back to doing what the earliest Christians did. So my tribe has paid a lot of attention to the book of Acts. But the more I've read Acts, the more I have realized how revolutionary this little book is. And how different the lives of the earliest Christians were from my own.

I don't know about you, but I live in a place in the world where being a Christian minister gives me a bit of an advantage. Most of the people around me give me a certain respect for being a leader in a movement they esteem.

It wasn't always that way.

In many times and places through the past (and in some places today), just being a Christian could mean a pretty certain death. It could mean to the authorities that you stood against the status quo, and they wouldn't stand for that. Many of those martyrs were just peasant men and women who were defying the most powerful kings and rulers of the world.

Behind all of this you won't find some revolutionary propaganda or an anarchist cookbook. You'll find a song. Mary's song.

Actually, it all starts with God, but he's a God who chooses to come to a teenage nobody named Mary. Luke describes her as a person of humility, but that word isn't so much referring to her attitude as it is to her position in society.

The word Luke uses means "oppressed by the misuse of power." She's on the lowest rung of the social ladder. In the affairs of her nation she doesn't have a voice, which makes it ironic that her voice is going to change the world.

With one sentence, this girl named Mary has her world turned upside down. An announcement from an angel absolutely blows her mind, because she's had that junior high biology class and knows that these things don't happen like that.

Instead of protesting, however, she opens her mouth and sings.

The Song of Death

Mary taps into Israel's greatest hits, the stories she grew up hearing, and she sets them to song. But not everyone appreciates this tune.

Listen to Mary's song:

My soul glorifies the Lord
    and my spirit rejoices in God my Savior,
for he has been mindful
    of the humble state of his servant.

From now on all generations will call me blessed,
for the Mighty One has done great things for me—
holy is his name.
His mercy extends to those who fear him,
from generation to generation.
He has performed mighty deeds with his arm;
he has scattered those who are proud in their
inmost thoughts.
He has brought down rulers from their thrones
but has lifted up the humble.
He has filled the hungry with good things
but has sent the rich away empty.
He has helped his servant Israel,
remembering to be merciful
to Abraham and his descendants forever,
even as he said to our fathers. (Luke 1:46–55)

Mary is announcing a social revolution. When Mary sings that the Lord has brought down rulers from their thrones, you're probably not too excited about that if you happen to occupy a throne.

Bible readers know that the king at the time is a dangerous, mentally ill old man named Herod the Great. He's a power broker who deals in tyranny. If he hears Mary's song, he is apt to try to shut her up, for Mary basically is announcing that this tyrant is about to get what's coming to him. So you can bet that he's not a fan of the newest hit.

But Luke keeps emphasizing this point: the Kingdom of God isn't always good news for smaller, self-centered kingdoms. Mary's song is a song of revolution. It signals doom for rulers who are opposing God's plans and his people. But, I wonder, how does she think this could possibly happen?

Mary is singing about God bringing down the rulers and lifting up the servants. What in the world does Mary think is going to happen?

Most revolutions are built upon the power of death. They require somebody to die. Ever since the Fall in Genesis 3, that's how the strong have subdued the weak. Because not dying has always served as a good incentive to keep people in line.

That's why, in the next chapter, right after Adam and Eve disobey the Lord, we are introduced to a guy named Lamech. When we first meet Lamech, he's singing.[4] He's singing about how he was willing to kill anyone who messed with him, up to seventy-seven times. What he's saying is that he will escalate any conflicts that people direct his way. He's the Tupac of the Old Testament.

If you were to ask Lamech, I'm sure he would have plenty of justification for his logic. He's not really a violence-prone man. He's just taking preventative measures. But the truth is, Lamech's way of life is contagious.

His tune is catchy and before long, everybody's singing it.

If you doubt this, all you have to do is watch CNN or Fox News. Human history is riddled with this song. Whoever has the biggest weapon wins. Only the strong survive. They control the world because ever since death entered the world, the fear of death has carried the day.

In the world Jesus is born into, Rome is in charge. They are changing the world; Caesar is bringing the *Pax Romana* to the entire world. The Shalom (or Peace) of the Garden is being replaced with the Peace of Rome.

They are trying to bring the Shalom that God intended, but they are using the strategy of Lamech.

According to the rumor going around when Jesus is born, the Romans will crucify people until they run out of space for the crosses and out of crosses for the bodies.

Caesar would have made Lamech proud.

Disturbed by the Resurrection

But death in not the only threat that those in power use to motivate their subjects. When we first see the early Christians getting in trouble with the law, the officials don't immediately threaten to kill them. They just try to incarcerate some sense into them.

> The priests and the captain of the temple guard and the Sadducees came up to Peter and John while they were speaking to the people. They were greatly disturbed because the apostles were teaching the people and proclaiming in Jesus the resurrection of the dead. They seized Peter and John, and because it was evening, they put them in jail until the next day. (Acts 4:1–3)

I love this passage. Those Temple officials are "disturbed" by the resurrection. They had murdered Jesus, so they don't want to hear another word from Jesus' people about his resurrection. After all, the Sadducees have been anti-resurrection for three or four generations, so they are determined to squelch any hint that anybody could expect to live again after death. Any discussion of resurrection is taboo in the Temple they control . . . not because the Sadducees are worried about some future hope, but because they are worried about *right now*.

The resurrection should be disturbing for some. It's not about going to some disembodied heaven. Sometimes we talk about resurrection as though it means we're going to go to some sterile place, white and clean, with soft music playing.

Most of us have heard of a heaven that looks like one of those Progressive Insurance commercials. But the Scriptures talk about resurrection—not about God getting us out of here, but about God setting this world right. Turning it into a place where there will be no more poverty, no injustice, no suffering.

The truth is, though, if the current system works for you, you may not like God's new way of doing this.

These officials didn't.

They put the apostles in jail, supposedly for healing a lame man. Which is kind of surprising. I always thought that helping people to walk again was a good thing. But the real crime is what Peter told the crowd about this healed man walking by the power of the risen Christ. Resurrection is what ticks them off.

So the religious leaders are hoping to put a good scare into Peter and John to get them to back down after spending the night in the can.

But jail is not going to stop Peter. He has learned his lesson about backing down. Now he stands on trial before the same court that sent Jesus to a cross, but Peter makes it clear that this trial is a sham. "If we're on trial for kindness," he begins his defense. It's a bit of a backhanded comment.

So the religious leaders go back and forth with the apostles, threatening with whatever it will take to get them to stop talking.

But what Peter says next is brilliant.

"You do what you have to do," Peter tells them. "You can beat us, imprison us, or even kill us, but we are not going to back down. We have a higher calling to God. Jesus has sent us through the whole world, and we take orders only from him."

This is not your normal revolution. Peter is submitting to their laws, but not obeying them. He admitted that some laws require punishment, but he believes that his calling from God is so important that he must accept whatever punishment goes with it.

What we see here is the beginning of a major theme in Christian history—the theme of civil disobedience.

Before we move on, look at what is fueling this whole scene:

> Repent, then, and turn to God, so that your sins may be wiped out, that times of refreshing may come from the Lord, and that he may send the Christ, who has been appointed for you—even Jesus. He must remain in heaven until the time comes for God *to restore everything,* as he promised long ago through his holy prophets. (Acts 3:19–21, emphasis mine)

The Restoration of All Things

I have witnessed a lot of church fights in my life. That is seldom a pretty sight; but the worst part of the problem is that what we fight about is usually so small.

When I was just eleven or twelve years old, my parents were going to a smaller church of about a hundred people. One Sunday night they held a business meeting and my dad dragged me along. I was getting pretty bored at church, so maybe he was thinking this would help me to appreciate it more. If I could see how the sausage was made, maybe that would spice up how I saw our community of faith.

He was right.

At some point in that meeting my dad suggested helping one of the widows of our church, but he didn't know that there was already some history between this widow and some of the men there. He found out!

Immediately he encountered stiff opposition. The next thing I knew, I saw a seventy-year-old man taking off his coat and yelling at my father, "I used to be a Golden Glove champion. I could beat your hide then, and I bet I still can!"

And as a twelve-year-old boy, I sat there thinking, *Now this is church!*

We religious people fight over the pettiest things. I've seen us fight over whether to have kitchens in church buildings, what color pews to have, what kind of songs we should sing, or whether or not we can have drums. I've noticed that people who are looking for a fight do so because they're not already engaged in a bigger one.

The earliest Christians are attempting to join God in the repair of the world. A calling so big they are willing to give their lives for it.

I'm a part of something called the Restoration Movement. This means we are trying to restore the early church, and that's a beautiful idea. But let me tell you, I don't think it's possible to restore the early church unless we restore what the early church cared about.

Their goal was the restoration of all things.

This means our story is bigger than we ever thought possible. It's about every square inch of creation. And maybe that explains what the apostles do next.

The Boldest Prayer Ever

After they are released from jail, Peter and John go back and report to everyone what had happened, and then they pray the last thing we would expect:

> "Sovereign Lord," they said, "you made the heaven and the earth and the sea, and everything in them. You spoke by the Holy Spirit through the mouth of your servant, our father David:

'Why do the nations rage
   and the peoples plot in vain?
The kings of the earth take their stand
   and the rulers gather together
against the Lord
   and against his Anointed One.'

Indeed Herod and Pontius Pilate met together with the Gentiles and the people of Israel in this city to conspire against your holy servant Jesus, whom you anointed. They did what your power and will had decided beforehand should happen. Now, Lord, consider their threats and enable your servants to speak your word with great boldness." (Acts 4:24–29)

"Sovereign Lord . . . ." Maybe we should start all our prayers like this. Remember they have just got out of prison, and they have been warned to stop speaking about Jesus. If this were my prayer, it might sound like, "Thank you God for delivering us from that close call. We now know this city isn't fertile ground."

But Peter and John don't pray for deliverance. They pray for boldness.

What do you pray when you realize that everything you've been asking for in the past has been against God's will? They had probably spent most of their lives praying for the world around them to be safe. "God, please don't let them arrest Jesus. Don't let them crucify him." But the resurrection turned everything upside down.

In this moment, the apostles realize something that changed everything. They realize that Pilate and Caesar think they alone are in control. They think they are calling the shots, but in reality they are doing exactly what God had foreordained.

God brought down the rulers and raised up the servant.

So now when those first Christians are threatened, they don't try to tell God what to do. They don't ask him to take away the threat. They have stopped praying prayers like that because they realize that God is up to something far bigger than their personal safety.

Back there in Eden, do you know what the first emotion was after the Fall? Fear. And it has ruled the day ever since.

In 1933, the young German pastor Martin Niemöller was invited to a delegation of church leaders to meet with the Nazi regime. When he was reflecting on it later he said, "I discovered that Herr Hitler is a terribly frightened man."[5]

We are afraid of so many things. We fear the unknown. We fear differences. We fear the dark. Some of us fear high places or open places or public places. There are people who actually are afraid of bald people.

Now fear isn't all bad. When your mammogram comes back positive, you ought to be afraid. When a tornado is bearing down on your home, you should be afraid.

But the one thing the early apostles learned from the life of Jesus is that even our suffering is redemptive. The things that threaten us the most may be the way God is able to work the most.

The Death of Death

The very thing that had paralyzed the apostles before the resurrection they now see as an opportunity for God to work. Death has been defeated. Lamech's code for life has been weighed and found wanting. And so we find that the fear of death no longer works to control people who believe that death has ultimately been defeated.

And in one of the most amazing verses in the Bible, we see the Temple leaders described like this: "After further threats they let them go. They could not decide how to punish them, because all the people were praising God for what had happened" (Acts 4:21).

They couldn't decide how to punish them.

I like the way N. T. Wright talks about how the resurrection changed these earliest days of the Jesus movement: "Death is the last Weapon of the Tyrant, and the point of the resurrection, despite much misunderstanding, is that death has been defeated. Resurrection is not the re-description of death; it is its overthrow and, with that, the overthrow of those whose power depends on it."[6]

An Anglican bishop many years ago made this statement, "Everywhere the early Christians went they started a riot. Everywhere I go they serve tea."[7]

I'd like to suggest that all churches add a line to our pamphlets, to our signs, and to our bylaws. I'd like to suggest that congregations everywhere add a phrase to all their announcements and greetings. When we collect the tithes for the week or ask people to sign up for a ministry or a mission trip, I think we ought to supplement our ministries with a five-word challenge:

SUPPORT YOUR LOCAL JESUS REVOLUTION.

If Christians today are not saying something like this, we may forget what story we are a part of. From the earliest Christians to the abolitionists of the 1800s to the Civil Rights movement of the 1960s and the fight against apartheid in South Africa, Christ's followers have been leading some kind of revolution. The gospel has been advancing when women and men put real skin on various forms of resurrection hope.

As Martin Luther King Jr. said, "There is nothing more tragic than to sleep through a revolution."

That's why it's appropriate that this story in Acts 4 ends the way it does. Tucked in this little prayer of boldness is a song. I like to think the apostles actually sang it. The song is Psalms 2, a royalty song (like "Hail to the Chief"), and the apostles properly apply it to Jesus. After all, he's the King. God has brought down rulers from their thrones and raised up the lowly, just as Mary told us in her song.

Luke starts his two-volume work by telling us about a peasant girl's song. Mary didn't start this revolution, but it was recognized by her and countless others who tune in to what God is doing.

On May 27, 1992, twenty-two innocent people were killed while waiting in line at a bakery in the capital city of Bosnia. They were waiting in the line at one of the few "safe places" in their country when a sudden bombing cut their lives short. What makes this story compelling is what happened the next day. Vedran Smailović, the cellist of the local opera, put on his black-tailed tuxedo and went to the site of the bombing, where he began to play Albinoni's *Adagio in G Minor.*

For the next three weeks, Smailović would play throughout his war-ravaged city. In honor of each of the victims of violence, he fought against the tragedy of war with the only weapon he had: a song.

He played for funerals, despite their tendency to be targeted by the snipers; he played in graveyards and in the streets. "I never stopped playing music throughout the siege. . . . My weapon was my cello."

Armed with only a song, he took on an army.[8] Which on many levels is what is happening in the story of Acts.

In this story the apostles are putting flesh on the very thing that Mary sang about decades earlier. Maybe this is why we find Paul and Silas singing in a Philippian jail cell at midnight. When the powers of Rome had done the worst they could imagine, Mary sang a song that disturbs the comfortable and comforts the disturbed.

It still does.

Did you know that tyrants in South America have made it illegal to sing Mary's song? Evidently they understand what she's singing about. Here's a girl who's got more than a tune. She's got a fire in her belly (and a Messiah, too), and she hopes in a God who is about to end the curse of Eden and restore all things to their original, intended design.

This is no lullaby Mary's singing. It's a song of deep hope for God to repair the world. When Mary sings, of course, none of this has happened yet. She's hoping, yearning for the day when everything is made right.

Spurred by that hope, she partners with God in bringing it to be.

And I have this notion that this is exactly what God wants to do through all of us. In the words of Barbara Brown Taylor, if you are Mary, "you can decide to be a daredevil, a test pilot. You can decide to take part in a plan that you did not choose, doing things that you do not know how to do for reasons you do not entirely understand. You can take part in a thrilling and dangerous scheme with no script and no guarantees. You can agree to smuggle God into the world inside your own body."[9]

Mary's story is our story, too. Her dream is the dream of God. The call of the church is for us to partner with God in setting the world right. For us to tune in to the song God is singing. The song that those who have gone before us are singing.

It is for us to smuggle God into the world through our own bodies.

We call it church, but I like to say, "Support your local Jesus revolution."

Chapter 2

The Bread
Back Home

"When he came to his senses, he said, 'How many of my father's hired servants have food to spare, and here I am starving to death!'

"But the father said to his servants, 'Let's have a feast and celebrate. For this son of mine was dead and is alive again.'"

—Luke 15:17, 22–24

As I was growing up, one of my best friends was Brian. He was a teenager with Down syndrome who was a few years older than me. Since I was homeschooled and went to a tiny church where Brian and I made up the entire "youth group," Brian and I were destined to be friends.

Every time the church met, Brian would lead a few songs. I say Brian would lead, Mrs. Ruby would basically start the song and the rest of us would join in. Brian just picked out the song and stood up front.

Eventually, we started asking Brian to pray the benediction (the closing prayer), and without fail he would always talk to God about food. Specifically, he would tell God what restaurant he wanted us to take him to after worship, and he would tell God what he planned on ordering there.

So Brian's prayer sounded something like, "Dear God, thank you for Foy and Ruby and Jonathan and Donna, and thank you, God, that we are about to go to Taco Bell, and that I'm going to get a chalupa."

Basically, Brian placed his order to God. But we never stopped Brian from participating in church. And it was there that I learned something important about what it means to be the people of God who bear the image of God.

East of Eden

For at least the last hundred years, the first chapters of Genesis have stirred a hot debate. You and I have read the creation story through the lens of the cultural battles we were having. Part of our problem is that Genesis is not primarily trying to argue with Charles Darwin.

One danger is that, while discussing Darwin, we may reduce the Bible to one single conversation that actually is incredibly new in relation to the age of Genesis. The creation story was not written to be a biology textbook. In fact, the first few chapters of the Bible address an infinitely broader and more important subject.

When God creates humanity, he tells them something interesting. He gives them dominion; he allows them to rule over the earth. They are placed in charge and made to be co-regents in God's good creation.

In one of the most loaded verses in the Bible, Genesis tells us that humans were created in God's own image.[1]

Now that is a loaded phrase.

It's a phrase that comes from a common practice in the ancient Near East. For example, when the Pharaoh of Egypt conquered Palestine in 1700 B.C., he left an image of himself in the city of

Megiddo. This image represented that ancient king's authority, his covenant.

On the image itself the treaty was written. The image was the presence of Pharaoh in the land.

This may be the idea that Genesis is tapping into here.

To be made in God's image is to have his authority. It is to represent him to others and to represent others to him. The biblical word for this representative role is *priest*.

A Theology of Priests

When you and I think of a priest, chances are we have a pretty narrow view of what that means. We may think of Bing Crosby Christmas movies, or national pedophilia scandals, or at best a choice few men who serve in a particular religious tradition. But the term *priest* originally was not intended to refer to just a select few religious officials.

Originally, being a priest was the task God gave humans. We were created in God's image to reflect who he is. But that was before Genesis 3. You probably know this story. Adam and Eve were told they were free to do anything (and remember they were naked!), but they couldn't eat from the tree of the Knowledge of Good and Evil.

But they did. And the Bible says their eyes were opened. For the first time they experienced fear and shame. They were supposed to be priests, to show the world what God was like, but they failed. Just as all of us do.

God's pre-Eden dream would not be stopped, however. After the Fall, God gives this priestly calling to his chosen nation, Israel. He singles out the tribe of Levi and gives the office of the priesthood to that specific tribe.

These Levites will be the ones who bear the responsibility of reflecting God's presence to the nation of Israel, who, in turn, are to show God's presence to the world. So back in the day of the Old

Testament, if you want to be a priest, you can't just go up to the Temple and say, "Hey, I just got my priest school degree, so I'm ready."

The entry exam to priest-training school consists of only one question: "Who's your daddy?"

The purpose for a priest is highly significant. A priest put the divine on display. If you wanted to know more about a religion's god back in those days, you would go to their temple and watch the priest—what he does, how he acts.

When Israel's priests are first initiated into office, they go through an elaborate, impressive ordination ceremony designed to impress on the new priests that they are becoming more than they used to be. They are now representatives of the Divine.

This first ceremony is described in Leviticus 8. There we see the first priests are told to wait at the tent of meeting for seven days, because they are becoming a new creation. After that ceremony and that holy delay, the new priests are ready to testify to the life and the nature of God.

They served as a mirror to the world, showing everyone what God was like. But over and over again, Israel messed up. In fact, it's just two chapters later when the priesthood starts to unravel. They have this unique calling, and they fail to live up to it.

It was like the sin in the Garden of Eden happened over and over again.

So, in the years that follow, God repeatedly sends his people into exile. They go into captivity in Egypt, or Assyria, or Babylon. Just as in Eden, the people of God get sent away.

In the Garden, everything was as God intended. But Genesis, and most of the Old Testament, makes it clear that the people God made are not in Eden anymore.

They're in exile.

Life in Exile

Now exile is the opposite of God's calling someone.

To be in exile is to be obsolete, inadequate, irrelevant. It's to be on the margins of society with a memory of a time when you weren't. And that's where we find the people of God when the prophet Isaiah starts preaching to them. For the first thirty-nine chapters of Isaiah, the prophet is telling Israel how bad exile is going to be for them.

They are going to be slaves for someone else. They are going to be unknown. If the world was the Jackson Five, they would be Tito. But then all of a sudden, in Isaiah 40, everything changes. The prophet promises a day when everything will be different, a day when God is going to bring them back from exile and once again they will make a difference in the world.

God is going to resurrect Israel.

In a later time of exile, Ezekiel has a dream of resurrection for the entire people of God. Ezekiel and Isaiah agree. When God restores his people, it is going to be about more than just Israel. It is going to be about the entire world, "to the ends of the earth."[2]

Luke's Exile

It is interesting that the Gospel of Luke opens by letting us know right off the bat that everything is not as it should be. Luke tells us that Caesar and Herod are running the show.

And by telling us this, Luke is letting us know that the people of God are still in exile—still under the rule of foreigners. So the first characters we meet in Luke all seem to have the same concerns in mind. Think about when Anna meets Jesus in Luke's first chapter. She says, "Here is the one who will redeem Israel." They are still in exile.

We see this idea in other places in the Bible. Such as Nehemiah 9:36. God's people are home, but not really. They are just a shadow of who they were made to be.

You know what's really interesting about Luke's Gospel? It's about the lost.

But who's lost?

When Luke refers to the lost, he is referring to the people of Israel. These are the people who have grown up hearing the stories about Moses and Elijah but have just given up on it.

They were called to be God's people, to reflect who he is, to reflect the very image of God. They were called to be a nation of priests, but they have lost it. And now Jesus is on the scene looking for them. Throughout Luke's Gospel we see this.

In Luke 8 when Jesus heals the woman with the bleeding disease, notice she had been sick for twelve years. Pay attention to the number. Twelve, and she's a woman.

Now I believe that this story really happened, but I believe Jesus is using it as a parable as well. Remember when Jesus raises the little girl from the dead? How old was she? Twelve.

There it is again. Luke is telling us something. I think he is winking at us here, giving us clues about what God is up to in Jesus—he is redeeming his people from exile.

In Luke, Jesus also tells a story about a prodigal son who goes off to a far country, and when he comes back the father welcomes him back with open arms.

The entire Gospel of Luke is about Jesus bringing the people of God out of exile—out of the far country. The Gospel of Luke is about a God who is coming home. It's about a God who is inviting the whole world to come back home.

Maybe that is why Luke repeatedly tells us that Jesus is walking to Jerusalem. Every miracle, every sermon reported by Luke happens when Jesus is returning to Jerusalem.

Until Jesus comes, the direction of the Bible seems to be moving *away* from God, but not any longer. Jesus is headed to Jerusalem.

Death and Resurrection

Of course, Jerusalem is where Jesus is tried and killed. It's where Jesus stands up to the powers that hold Israel captive, and they kill him.

And the hopes of Israel seem to die when he does. That's where we find a couple of disciples right after Jesus dies. They are walking away from Jerusalem. They have given up on Jesus. They have given up on God using them. In their minds, Jesus was supposed to be the one who set everything right. He was supposed to be their Messiah, but now he has joined the long list of dead Messiahs.

"But we had hoped." Hope is sometimes the worst thing that can die, isn't it?

And so Jesus does the only thing that can restore their hope. He eats with them:

> As they approached the village to which they were going, Jesus acted as if he were going farther. But they urged him strongly, "Stay with us, for it is nearly evening; the day is almost over." So he went in to stay with them.
>
> When he was at the table with them, he took bread, gave thanks, broke it and began to give it to them. Then their eyes were opened and they recognized him, and he disappeared from their sight. They asked each other, "Were not our hearts burning within us while he talked with us on the road and opened the Scriptures to us?"

They got up and returned at once to Jerusalem. (Luke 24:28–33)

Throughout the Gospel of Luke, Jesus eats a lot, and almost always with the wrong people. Jesus seems to take great joy in eating with prostitutes and tax collectors and every person who found themselves on the outside looking in. Jesus seems to think that a good meal can be medicine for the soul. And now he's eating again.

N. T. Wright suggests that Luke is winking at the reader here, because the first time that we are told about people eating in the Bible is in Genesis 3, when Adam and Eve eat the forbidden fruit. When they eat it in Eden, their eyes are opened.[3]

And now Luke tells us that Jesus eats with these disciples and their eyes are opened. And once they realize what has happened, their immediate response *is to turn around.*

As in the prodigal son story, the exile is over. It's time to go home.

All this time, people have been headed away from the plans and purposes of God. But at the resurrection, everything is turned upside down. Including their travel plans. Which brings us finally to the book of Acts. Because Acts is the sequel, the "Empire Strikes Back" to the Gospel of Luke. And it is here that Luke shows us what it looks like when the people of God really are being the people of God. "But you will receive power when the Holy Spirit comes on you; and you will be my witnesses in Jerusalem, and in all Judea and Samaria, and to the ends of the earth" (Acts 1:8).

Just as Isaiah promised, God's people in Acts will go through the entire world, to the ends of the earth, telling the principalities and powers that Jesus is Lord. They will show the world what it looks like when people accept Jesus as their Lord.

They are witnesses to Jesus, they are witnessing to the divine, they are showing the world what God is like. Now it may be lost on us, but this just happens to be priestly language.

Jesus' followers are told to wait in Jerusalem, where they will be anointed with the Holy Spirit. They are finally reclaiming their vocation to show the world what God is like.

A few years ago, I was shooting a video for a church where I was working. The video was about the priesthood of all believers, and I was dressed up like a Catholic priest.

We had finished shooting the video, and I was driving around in downtown Fort Worth when I may have cut off a car. Needless to say, they weren't big fans of that. So this car sped around me and the driver gave me the universal sign for "I don't like you as a person." And then he saw how I was dressed. Apparently a collar covers a multitude of sins. In my mind I was thinking, "I'm not really a priest."

I drove to a 7/11 to grab a drink, and a man there held the door for me and said, "Go ahead, Father." Now I didn't want to take advantage of a religious tradition that I don't belong to, so I told him I wasn't a priest, that I was actually just shooting a video. But I thanked him anyway.

I walked to the fountain drink machine and another guy there told me, "After you, Father." So I explained the whole thing over again. Then I went to the counter to pay for my Diet Dr. Pepper, and the woman behind the counter said, "It's on the house for you, Father."

And I said, "Bless you, my child."

Don't judge me, it was a free drink.

One of the hardest things to do as a preacher is to convince other Jesus followers that we really are priests. One of the hardest things to do as a follower of Jesus is to convince myself that I am one.

Most of us can think of plenty of reasons why God can't use us, can't we? We know how broken, how not-priestly we are.

But Jesus has a gospel for all of us in exile.

So you had an abortion and maybe the rest of your life has been trying to get over that guilt. You don't have to be defined by that anymore. Ever since the divorce, you've been coasting along at church. You come, but you've checked out. It's time for you to realize that this is past. It's over. You're not in exile anymore.

So he's gone, or she's gone, and ever since you haven't been the same. Maybe you need to hear the resurrection of Jesus saying, "You're not in exile anymore."

So you and your spouse have always had this sense that you wanted to do something about the injustices you see. But you feel so inadequate. How could God use you? It's time to get over feeling inadequate and impotent. The Lord can do through you far more than anything you might ask or think. You're not in exile anymore.

If you belong to this story, then you are a part of a historical stream of broken people, people who have gathered together so that they can remind each other that Jesus is risen, and then go out and put flesh on that.

I like the way Jean Vanier says this: "A community is not simply a group of people who live together and love each other. It is a place of resurrection."[4]

The resurrection means that nothing will ever be the same. And that includes the way we think of ourselves and our calling. It did for the earliest Christians, and it can for us.

This is something I experienced firsthand growing up.

Brian, my friend with Downs syndrome, gave me a vision of the dream of God. I mentioned earlier that Brian always led a couple of songs and prayed the final prayer, but that's where it stopped. Since Brian's prayer tended to gravitate toward fast food, we didn't ask him to pray the important prayers—like for the Lord's Supper.

But not everyone knew our unspoken rules. One day, we had a visitor come worship with us, and we asked him to preside over the Lord's Supper. At this point, Brian was assisting in passing the plates, but he had never been asked to pray for communion. After all, we knew what those prayers sounded like. We didn't want the prayer for communion to mention Burger King.

But on this particular day, our visitor didn't know that. So after he had prayed for the bread, he turned to Brian and asked him to pray for the cup. Immediately, the other nine church members were thinking, "Nooooo."

And that's when it happened.

Brian bowed his head, and prayed twelve words that are forever seared in my memory. "God, thank you for the blood. I know it hurt you. Amen."

And my eyes were opened.

That's what Luke is trying to tell us. That is what the book of Acts is whispering to us wherever we are. You, in all your flaws, in all your brokenness, can be a part of this.

You're not in exile anymore.

This is why for two thousand years the people of God have gathered together to break bread and share wine. Different traditions know it by different names and celebrate it in different ways, but it's all the same story. We gather together with the risen Jesus, we name the evil in our own hearts and in the world, we confess, we worship, we break bread, and our eyes are opened.

Although life may be messy, we may have great obstacles, we can see a little more clearly that things weren't always this way, and they won't always be this way.

Our failures have been our fig leaves, but we can no longer hide behind them. If death enters the world when we sin, then resurrection is the forgiveness of sins. The resurrection story means we, in all our messiness, are invited back from exile. The resurrection means we are invited back to our original calling.

It's time to come home.

Chapter 3

The Prodigal
Preacher

"I fled Him, down the nights and down the days;
I fled Him, down the arches of the years;
I fled Him, down the labyrinthine ways
Of my own mind; and in the midst of tears.
I hid from Him.
But with unhurrying chase, and unperturbed pace,
Deliberate speed, majestic instancy.
The beat-and a voice beat-
More instant than the Feet-
'All things betray thee, who betrayest Me.'"

—Francis Thompson, "The Hound of Heaven"

"While he was still a long way off, his Father saw him."

—Luke 15:20

If you were to look up John Newton on Wikipedia, you would find out that he was a slave-trader for several years. He was someone who made money by trafficking fellow human beings. You would find out that eventually he repented of this great evil and became an Anglican minister and one of the great anti-slavery abolitionists.

You would also learn that Newton wrote the classic hymn, "Amazing Grace." But what most Church history courses won't tell you, what you will rarely hear in a sermon, is that he wrote that hymn *while he was still a slave-trader.*

The Call of Peter

One of the most famous passages in the entire New Testament, at least for a lot of us, is Acts 2. It's the first Day of Pentecost after Jesus rose from the dead. It's the day when the church began.

Did you ever wonder why Peter is the one who gives the sermon on that Pentecost morning? It's one of the most famous sermons in the Bible, and Peter has just gone through a rough stretch. It's fair to say that he's in the rehabilitation period, so it seems like someone else would have been more qualified to preach that day.

Before we can answer the question of why Peter gets pushed forward onto center stage that day, we've got to remember why Peter was there in the first place.

Back in Luke 5, Jesus calls his first disciples. They are fishermen, and they've been out fishing all night. When Jesus asks them how it went, they admit that they have not caught a thing. Not even a minnow.

Thus completing one of Jesus' most fantastic miracles—getting a fisherman to admit not catching anything.

When this Jewish carpenter shows up, he tells these exhausted fishermen to get back out on the water. To fish some more. Now these guys don't fish during the day. They fish at night. They are professionals. If they do what Jesus tells them to do, they know they're not going to catch anything but a sunburn, and Peter makes that clear. But then he says to Jesus, "Because you asked, I'll do it."

And they never look back. They catch so many fish that another boat has to come over and help haul them in. In five minutes they catch their monthly quota. So when Jesus follows up with a request for them to follow him, they do it.

But I don't think that Peter, Andrew, James, and John have any idea what kind of invitation this is. Jesus tells them him he'll make them "fishers of people." The fishermen don't know exactly what that means. I think that they just know that this guy knows more about their profession than they do. He obviously knows how to catch fish. So they follow him.

Now chances are that most of you reading this already know how this internship goes for Peter. He will spend the next three years learning one-on-one from God-in-the-flesh. And Peter is going to make a ton of mistakes. He gets reprimanded more than all the other apostles put together. Once Jesus even calls him Satan.

You haven't had a bad day until Jesus calls you Satan.

But the worst mistake Peter makes is one that he is even warned about. Near the end of his ministry, Jesus tells Peter that things are about to get ugly. That Rome is going to crucify him, and Peter is going to be the last one to deny him.

To his credit, Peter's not one to go down without a fight. When the Roman guards come to arrest Jesus, Peter is the one who whips out his sword to defend the Master. And you don't pull your sword on the Temple guards unless you're ready to die.

Instantly Jesus corrects him one last time. "Peter, put up your sword!" he says. And poor Peter, who doesn't have a clue what he should do at this point, watches as his world turns upside down. It becomes apparent that Jesus is about to be crucified. With death staring him and his comrades in the face, Peter turns into a coward. He denies Jesus three times, just as Jesus said he would. And John tells us that, after this, Peter abandons his ministry dreams and goes back home to his boat, back to fishing.

I know that most of us know what happens later in this story. But let's wait just a bit before we go there.

For Everyone Everywhere

Chances are your Bible calls Genesis 10 "The Table of Nations." It strikes me as one of the most boring chapters in the Bible. It makes genealogies look exciting.

Not long after Noah unloads the Ark, Genesis burns a whole chapter doing a roll call of nations. Why do we need this information? At least in part because the next story is about what happens when these nations come together.

As humans begin to repopulate Earth after the flood, they try to get together and build a tower to make a name for themselves. They overstep their bounds as created beings, so God does something to remind them that they are creatures and not the Creator.

He initiates a little project called "Let's Stop Talking." He ends their conversations mid-project by confusing their language. And the exact thing they were worried about—being scattered—happens to them.

And the very thing they want most—to make a name for themselves—they fail to achieve.

But the writers of Genesis have an agenda. They are telling us the story in a particular way. Because the next story is about a guy named Abraham.

What really interests me is what the Lord tells Abraham when he calls him. He will make his name great. Just what the tower-builders longed for. God tells Abraham he will be blessed so that he can become a blessing to the entire world. It was a promise Abraham would hang on to for the rest of his life, and so did the rest of his family.

Instead of seeing their sacrifices as a way to be forgiven, Jewish people in ancient times saw them as a way of reminding God of his promise to Abraham. That covenant—that promise—marked them forever as God's chosen nation.

Each day the Jews would sacrifice lambs at 9 A.M. and at 3 P.M., in part to remember that God was going to use them, the family of Abraham, to be a blessing to the world.

Which brings us back to the book of Acts.

All of us have times when we wish we could turn the clock backwards—reverse the calendar—in order to undo something or unmake some decision we now regret. But time doesn't work like that, and life is all too unforgiving for this common human condition.

At least we thought it was.

Because the life, death, and resurrection of the Son of God have initiated a far more compelling plan of God. One that requires that his human creatures be able to communicate with each other again.

When the day of Pentecost came, they were all together in one place. Suddenly a sound like the blowing of a violent wind came from heaven and filled the whole house where they were sitting. They saw what seemed to be tongues of fire that separated and came to rest on each of them. All of them were filled with the Holy Spirit and began to speak in other tongues as the Spirit enabled them.

Now there were staying in Jerusalem God-fearing Jews from every nation under heaven. When they heard this sound, a crowd came together in bewilderment, because each one heard them speaking in his own language. Utterly amazed, they asked: "Are not all these men who are speaking Galileans? Then how is it that each of us hears them in his own native language? Parthians, Medes and Elamites; residents of Mesopotamia, Judea and Cappadocia, Pontus and Asia, Phrygia and Pamphylia,

Egypt and the parts of Libya near Cyrene; visitors from
Rome (both Jews and converts to Judaism); Cretans and
Arabs—we hear them declaring the wonders of God in
our own tongues!" Amazed and perplexed, they asked one
another, "What does this mean?"

Some, however, made fun of them and said, "They
have had too much wine." (Acts 2:1–13)

When the crowd at the Temple that Pentecost Day hear the apostles
speaking the span of human languages, they can't believe their ears.
They want to know how unschooled men from a backwater province
can speak the languages of the entire civilized world.

That's what is happening. Right here, Acts offers us a long list
of nations.

And the list is not random. Acts is doing exactly what Genesis 10
did. The first time the Bible gives us a roll call of nations, it is in the
context of the story of the Tower of Babel. And now God is reversing
it. No longer will language separate humans. Now God is drawing
us together again.

Andy Crouch talks about how momentous this moment is for
the birth of Christianity:

Most Jewish people would have grown up referring to "the
nations" . . . with disdain. But now "the nations" in all their
variety were to be offered the same message of faith and
repentance as Israel. Nations was now a word of inclusion,
not exclusion. . . . There is no culture beyond its reach-be-
cause the very specific cultural story of Israel was never anything other than a rescue mission for all the cultures of the
world, initiated by the world's Creator.[1]

What's going on here in Acts 2 is huge. The curse of Babel is reversed, Abraham's promise is being fulfilled, and Peter is speaking. But what happened to Peter to bring him here at this moment for this critical sermon?

Remember Peter had gone back to his old job. He had gone back to fishing. And we all know what it's like to go back to fishing.

He had failed. Worse than he ever imagined he could. It seems obvious to Peter that his part in the story that God is telling in Jesus is over. So Peter goes back to what he did before Jesus called him. Just as if that Jesus part of his life had never happened

Peter had lived three years with Jesus, hearing him tell stories about prodigals coming home and hookers being forgiven. But, at the time, surely Peter thought that teaching didn't apply to him.

I think Peter is fishing because he thinks he blew it. He had the chance to do something great and when the moment came, he screwed it all up. So he's sitting there wishing he would have done it all differently.

Jesus has defeated death. The entire cosmos has shifted when Jesus is resurrected. Everything has changed except Peter.

If you had asked Peter if he believed Jesus had risen from the dead, I'm sure he would have given an orthodox answer. But he—maybe like us—would have assumed that it had nothing to do with him.

And so we find Peter thinking all hope is lost, but at least the fish are biting. Right then Jesus shows up to reconnect with Peter, to let him know that he hasn't given up on the fisherman. Jesus still has plans for his life.

This story should be nothing but encouraging for every Jesus follower. Few of us will mess up our lives as bad as Peter did that day by the fire. Jesus didn't walk away from the one who walked away from him, and he won't turn his back on us.

Jesus welcomes a guilty Peter back into the ministry he has trained him to fulfill. He still wants Peter to feed his sheep. When he reaffirms his fallen apostle, Jesus shows him that resurrection is not just about changing cosmic problems such as defeating death. Resurrection is incredibly personal. It means new life for sinners like Peter. For sinners like you and me.

So, in Acts 2 we find Peter standing up in front of thousands of people. We hear him boldly preaching about the man he denied just a few weeks before. From a text in the book of Joel he preaches a message about restoration. About how things can be made right when we have totally messed up. Which is something that Peter now knows more than a little something about.

Peter is the prodigal come home.

The International League of the Guilty

Which brings me back to John Newton. He wrote the song "Amazing Grace" before he quit the slave trade. He wrote it as a religious person who was blind to the grave evil he was currently involved in, but eventually that grace drove him to face it.

And when he did, the grace that drove his heart to fear also drove him to give his life to fight for the freedom of others.[2]

Acts talks about Abraham more than any other book in the New Testament. There's a reason that Luke is going to great lengths to plug the story of the early church into the story of Abraham.

Part of the reason is because new religions were illegal at that time. Rome didn't want a lot of new religions springing up. This could be one reason why Luke is showing that Christianity isn't a new thing. It actually is something older than civilization itself.

But the other reason, and I would argue, the bigger reason, is what God promised through Abraham—to bless the entire world. This is precisely what the early church is taught to care about.

Remember how Luke introduces us to Peter?

In his Gospel, Luke tells us about Jesus calling Peter right after they catch a boatload of fish. And Jesus tells Peter that if he will follow him, he'll make that fisherman a fisher of people.

This is the promise Jesus made to Peter three years before that dramatic scene in Acts 2. This time it's not fish in the net. This time Peter preaches the first sermon for the church and three thousand people find God.

Do you see what this means? Peter's life still can count for something bigger than just Peter's life. The truth is that God doesn't bring back Peter for Peter's sake. He does it for the sake of the entire world. He saves Peter for purposes much larger than Peter. And now Peter doesn't just have a message. Now Peter *is* a message.

This is what it looks like to have your sins forgiven. This is what it looks like to see the prodigal coming home.

This chapter opened with a quote from one of the most famous Christian poems in the past hundred years. You probably know it: "The Hound of Heaven." But what you might not know is that the poem's author, Francis Thompson, was a desperate opium addict for most of his adult life.

He constantly struggled with his addiction, got kicked out of public libraries for his appearance, begged for money to get a fix. Once he attempted suicide and was nursed back to health by a prostitute, to finally die, after one more relapse into his addiction, at the young age of forty-eight.

This is the man who told the world of the "Hound of Heaven." In describing Thompson, G. K. Chesterton said about his poem, "[It] is as much an event of history, as an event of literature. Those who best understand the world know that the world is changed; and that the hunt [of the Hound of Heaven] will continue until the world turns to bay."

Do you see why Peter is the one speaking on that Pentecost morning? What God does with Peter that day is what he wants to do with all of us.

His purposes are bigger than us, but they include us! Not in spite of our shortcomings and failures, but through them. After all, only someone who runs can tell us about a God who chases.

Francis Spufford calls the church "The International League of the Guilty." And I think that, judging from how the church began in Acts 2, that's about as good a description as you can get. The church is filled with men and women who don't just have a message, but who are the message.

This is grace that really is amazing.

The Hound of Heaven is on the move.

Chapter 4

Calling All
Prophets

*"There was a time when the church was very powerful—in the time
when the early Christians rejoiced at being deemed worthy to suffer
for what they believed. In those days the church was not merely
a thermometer that recorded the ideas and principles of popular
opinion; it was a thermostat that transformed the mores of society.
Whenever the early Christians entered a town, the people in power
became disturbed and immediately sought to convict the Christians
for being 'disturbers of the peace' and 'outside agitators.' But the
Christians pressed on. . . . Things are different now. So often the
contemporary church is a weak, ineffectual voice with an uncertain
sound. So often it is an arch defender of the status quo. Far from
being disturbed by the presence of the church, the power structure of
the average community is consoled by the church's silent—and often
even vocal—sanction of things as they are."*

—Dr. Martin Luther King Jr., "Letter from a Birmingham Jail"

Recently, I was driving through a fast-food drive-thru when I
saw a bumper sticker on the vehicle in front of me. It was a
quote from the Roman philosopher Seneca, who said, "Religion is
regarded by the common people as true, by the wise as false, and by
the rulers as useful."[1]

I live in West Texas, and Taco Bueno is not normally where I go for profound ideas. Nobody ever says, *I'd like a tostada and a side of Socrates.* But I very much understand this quote. The dark side of religion, the part we don't talk about, is that it can be misused by mis-leaders to maintain the status quo. It is, as Karl Marx said, "the opium of the masses."

When I talk to my friends who are leaving their churches and giving up on following Jesus, I've learned that some of them have heard the message that Christianity is basically saying something like: Sure the world stinks right now, but if you just wait until you die, then everything will get sorted out.

For the past hundred years in some theological circles, resurrection has been misrepresented as a doctrine that promotes indifference. Somewhere along the way this core truth of Christianity changed from a revolutionary story to one that maintains the status quo. We started hearing the resurrection of Jesus presented as a way of saying, "If you just wait 'til you die, things will get better. So don't rock the boat now."

But Acts offers us a different idea about what resurrection means. It's not this idea that endorses the way things are. Instead it is a story about a person, and a hope that what God did for that person is going to happen for the entire world.

Some of the riots in Acts are directly tied to Jesus' followers preaching the resurrection. Because the resurrection isn't always seen as a good thing. If the status quo works for you, if the world benefits you, you might not like the idea of a God who is turning the world upside down.

"The last shall be first" sounds great for those who are at the back of the line; but if you are at the top of the food chain, it sounds a lot more like a threat.

The resurrection was, and still is, a revolutionary doctrine. It doesn't just mean that death no longer has the final word. It is so much bigger than that. Resurrection is about God setting the entire world right. It is the energy that has sustained and fed the people of God for centuries.

Especially the prophets.

The Role of a Prophet

The prophet's role in the Old Testament was not a popular one. Not a lot of little kids dreamed of growing up to be a prophet. Prophets weren't exactly the Spiderman of the day. In fact, most prophets were only appreciated posthumously.

But the world needed prophets. And here's why.

In 1 Kings we read about a king named Ahab who lives next door to a fellow named Naboth. Naboth just happens to have a vineyard, a fine vineyard that has been handed down in his family for generations.

Ahab begins to covet that property. Ahab approaches Naboth and offers him a good price for the vineyard. But Naboth says No. No amount of cajoling will make him sell. So Ahab gets all mopey and upset. That's where his wife Jezebel finds him when she comes home. He's sulking like a third-grader. When she finds out what the problem is, Jezebel reminds Ahab that he is the King of Israel, and tells him "Cheer up! I'll get you that vineyard."[2]

Jezebel's premise is that a king can take whatever he wants. So she sets up false witnesses to lie and say that Naboth had been blaspheming. Naboth gets stoned, and Ahab gets his vineyard.

Sounds like a happy ending, right?

But Ahab and Jezebel have not counted on one thing. A prophet named Elijah. Elijah comes to confront Ahab, telling him, "God is about to wreck your world for what you did to Naboth." Which probably sounds normal to us. If a king acts unjustly, God enforces justice. But that's not the way it used to be.

When a king did something in ancient times, it was the job of the gods (at least, the job of that king's god) to legitimize it, to justify it. (This is why they used the blasphemy charges to get the vineyard.)

But the God of Israel is a different kind of God, and he is trying to set humanity on a different path. One where those in power don't lord it over others. This God doesn't exist just to legitimize existing power structures; he actually calls them to be accountable.

To some people, that's a new idea, even though it seems as if it should have been around forever.

In fact, according to the Scriptures, if you are in power, God holds you more accountable. The prophets exist to remind us that God is larger than our power structures. When we humans get too big for our own britches, the prophets remind us that we answer to someone else.

One more thing about Naboth: He is the only person in the Old Testament who is stoned unjustly. But he isn't the last just man stoned in the Bible. In Acts 6 and 7, we find a story that kind of parallels Naboth's. It's about a man named Stephen.

> Now Stephen, a man full of God's grace and power, did great wonders and miraculous signs among the people. Opposition arose, however, from members of the Synagogue of the Freedmen (as it was called)—Jews of Cyrene and Alexandria as well as the provinces of Cilicia and Asia. These men began to argue with Stephen, but they could not stand up against his wisdom or the Spirit by whom he spoke.
>
> Then they secretly persuaded some men to say, "We have heard Stephen speak words of blasphemy against Moses and against God."

So they stirred up the people and the elders and the teachers of the law. They seized Stephen and brought him before the Sanhedrin. They produced false witnesses, who testified, "This fellow never stops speaking against this holy place and against the law. For we have heard him say that this Jesus of Nazareth will destroy this place and change the customs Moses handed down to us."

All who were sitting in the Sanhedrin looked intently at Stephen, and they saw that his face was like the face of an angel. (Acts 6:8–15)

I know this story sounds weird. This guy gets backed into a corner and his noggin starts glowing. Which is unusual. Bible characters don't often transfigure into Tinkerbell. But one of the things going on here is that the Jewish people in power are worried that they are going to lose their power.

So they start claiming that they are the true Jewish faith and this group of Jesus' followers are imposters. Specifically, they claim that Stephen is speaking words of blasphemy against Moses and God.

That's when Stephen's face starts glowing. Which is like an immediate conversation stopper, because these people know their Bibles. They know about the time in Exodus 34 when Moses had been up on Mount Sinai with God. You may remember that strange story. When Moses came down off the mountain, he looked like a glowworm. His face was so shiny that the people he was leading were terrified.

Stephen's enemies know this story, so they probably understand what God is showing them here. They are accusing Stephen of being against Moses, and suddenly he starts looking like him.

But they just keep on attacking Stephen.

The Story of Subversion

They ask Stephen if their charges against him are true, and Stephen responds by saying, "Once upon a time . . . ."

> Then the high priest asked him, "Are these charges true?"
> To this he replied: "Brothers and fathers, listen to me!
> The God of glory appeared to our father Abraham while
> he was still in Mesopotamia, before he lived in Haran."
> (Acts 7:1–2)

When I was fourteen, my parents sent me to stay for a week with some of our extended family in Russellville, Arkansas. Which is about ten miles from the edge of the earth.

To give you some kind of context, I grew up on a farm with goats and sheep and well-water, and these particular relatives called us "city folks." They are great people, though. They raise horses and live on a huge tract of land.

At one point that week, they decided they were going to have some fun with me. They were going to teach me how to ride a horse. So they put me on this one horse that looked kind of gentle but had apparently been secretly possessed with an evil spirit. About five minutes into the ride, I suddenly found myself flying through the air and landing flat on my back.

Not being one to give up easily, I climbed back on my bucking bronco to show this mare who is boss. Apparently that was her agenda, too. Not thirty seconds went by before I was back on the ground, wheezing for breath and wondering why cows are the main ingredient in hamburgers.

While that was not a pleasant experience, it did make a great story. When I got back home, I told all my friends about getting off this massive beast of a horse. But what I failed to tell my friends, and what I haven't told you yet, is that the horse I had been riding was actually . . . a Shetland pony.

The way I told the story to my family, they would have thought that I had been bucked off Sea Biscuit.

We all tell stories with a slant. We emphasize certain things and minimize or leave out others. That's exactly what Stephen is doing. He retells the story of Israel, but he tells it in a particular way. He is going to emphasize Abraham, and then Joseph and Moses and David. And here's why.

Stephen is being accused of blaspheming the Temple. Stephen reminds them that in their own history, God showed up to people and in places outside of the Temple. God is not confined to expensive, elaborate buildings. God does just fine revealing himself in burning bushes or deserts.

The second point Stephen makes is even more powerful. He retells the story of Israel, but he emphasizes times in their history when the so-called religious leaders of the day rejected someone through whom God was actually working. Joseph was rejected by his brothers. Moses was rejected, twice, by the very people he was trying to lead out of captivity.

The point Stephen is making here is huge!

He's telling them their own narrative and letting them know that they are playing the wrong parts. This may explain why he ends his sermon the way he does. He calls them stiff-necked people, with uncircumcised hearts and ears, which in my experience is not a good way to endear yourself to the audience. And then he asks one of the most provocative questions in the entire Bible: "Was there ever a prophet that your fathers didn't persecute?"

Did you know that, except for a few isolated incidents, prophets always were sent to the people of God? Prophets were sent to let them know they had wandered off track somehow. And it hardly ever went over well.

Religious people did not usually respond, "Okay, you're right. We're sorry." Instead, they figured out that the best way to silence the prophets was by killing them. And they did.

Jesus refers to this in Matthew 23:29–30 when he is talking to the religious leaders of his day: "You build tombs for the prophets and decorate the graves of the righteous. And you say, 'If we had lived in the days of our forefathers, we would not have taken part with them in shedding the blood of the prophets.'"

Modern-Day Prophets

After Martin Luther King Jr. gave his famous "I Have a Dream" speech, he was immediately blacklisted by the FBI as the most dangerous black man in the country. They suspected he was a communist.

Today we celebrate his birthday as a federal holiday.

We decorate the tombs of prophets.

But it's not the wrong action of the government in those civil rights days that disturbs me so much as it is the inaction of the church. Dozens of times I've read Dr. King's letter to white clergy, a letter written from his Birmingham jail cell, and every time it haunts me. I've often wondered why the people of God so easily accept and maintain the status quo.

This line from Jesus is one of the most convicting things Jesus says to me. I'm religious. I've grown up in church. I love the Lord and believe the Lord loves me. And that's exactly the crowd Jesus is talking to in Matthew 23. To them, to me, Jesus doesn't just say your ancestors did this, but he points out that they would have probably done it had they been alive. For the last few years a question has haunted me. I wonder what I would have done if I had been alive in 1960. And if I'm honest, I think I would have fought against civil rights.

Because I know me. I know how easy it is for me to play the wrong character in my own story. That's why we need prophets, even though we don't always appreciate them.

Notice the way the story of Stephen ends:

> When they heard this, they were furious and gnashed their teeth at him. But Stephen, full of the Holy Spirit, looked up to heaven and saw the glory of God, and Jesus standing at the right hand of God. "Look," he said, "I see heaven open and the Son of Man standing at the right hand of God."
>
> At this they covered their ears and, yelling at the top of their voices, they all rushed at him, dragged him out of the city and began to stone him. Meanwhile, the witnesses laid their clothes at the feet of a young man named Saul. (Acts 7:54–58)

I love this. They cover their ears and start yelling! How mature. What's next? I'm rubber and you're glue? And tucked in the middle of their murdering is a little detail about Stephen seeing Jesus.

Being a prophet has lots of downsides—like being hated and disliked, even being murdered. But for all the negatives, the one profit to being a prophet is that you get to see God. Think about it—Ezekiel, Isaiah, Jeremiah, and now Stephen.

The heavens open up and Stephen sees Jesus. It's a heavenly court scene. And that's significant, because Stephen is currently in court. He's on trial for his life.

At the moment of condemnation by that earthly court, however, Stephen gets a vision of that heavenly one. One in which he is loved and commended. In the middle of a ton of scowls, he knows he's made God smile. This is something the prophets know that we tend to forget—that if God is smiling at you, all other opinions are inconsequential. The life of a prophet may be hard and short, but it's worth it to get to see God.

That's what I think gives Stephen the power to end his life on a note of grace and faith.

> While they were stoning him, Stephen prayed, "Lord Jesus, receive my spirit." Then he fell on his knees and cried out, "Lord, do not hold this sin against them." When he had said this, he fell asleep. (Acts 7:59–60)

Stephen has just seen Jesus, the embodiment of resurrection, so he's not concerned about what they can do to him. As Dr. King said before he died, there is a certain kind of fire that no water hoses can put out.

Did you see the way that this story ends? Luke tells us, "He fell asleep."

Prophets Never Die

This is the point of the resurrection. Prophets never die! Can you see the power that Stephen has found here? He knows that even if God allows him to die, it will not be in vain. And it isn't, because right there in this murderous crowd is a guy named Saul.

The very guy who is going to spread the gospel to the entire world, we first meet while he's participating in a murder. If you have read Acts, you know that he later will be named Paul, and he's going to write more about the resurrection than any other New Testament writer.

He first sees the power of it right here.

Years later, in his letters, when Paul refers to the saints who have died in Christ, do you know what his favorite term is for death? Sleep.

Death is so final and injustice is so permanent, unless you believe in the resurrection. In that case, death is just a nap.

Archeologists have discovered a first-century sign in Jerusalem that warns people not to steal bodies from graves. I can imagine why that was necessary. If one guy missing from his grave causes so much ruckus, they don't want it ever to happen again. But they couldn't stop it! The fuel for the book of Acts is the undeniable fact that death had been defeated.

And that is still the fuel for the church.

I love the last public words Dr. King ever spoke. On the night before he was assassinated, in his final speech, he said:

> Well, I don't know what will happen now. We've got some difficult days ahead. But it doesn't matter with me now. Because I've been to the mountaintop. And I don't mind. Like anybody, I would like to live a long life. Longevity has its place. But I'm not concerned about that now. I just want to do God's will. And he's allowed me to go up to the mountain. And I've looked over. And I've seen the promised land. I may not get there with you. But I want you to know tonight, that we, as a people, will get to the promised land. And I'm happy tonight. I'm not worried about anything. I'm not fearing any man. Mine eyes have seen the glory of the coming of the Lord.[3]

That's remarkable. He feared no one. This was the last speech Dr. King ever gave; he was shot in Memphis the next day. His reward for living a life that was not dominated by fear. But in so many ways, the influence of his life was just beginning.

The same hope and faith in the risen Lord that sustained Stephen in his final hour gave peace and calm to Dr. King on that last day. The resurrection is still what animates and sustains prophets everywhere. This dangerous idea doesn't belong just to apostles and visionary civil rights leaders. The heart of Acts is this grand message that the hope and strength of resurrection are God's gift for everyone.

Calling All Prophets

Do you know who Stephen was?

Right before the Acts 7 story of his death, we read about a time when the apostles feel overwhelmed with people needing help. Widows need to be fed and food needs to be distributed, and the folks in one minority group are fussing because their widows don't appear to be getting their fair share.

The apostles tell the complainers it's not right for the Twelve to stop preaching the gospel to wait on tables, so they pick seven guys to deal with the feeding and the fussing.

Stephen is one of them. He is, in the words of the apostles, a waiter.

You'd probably never have known his name, and people wouldn't name their little boys Stephen if this had not happened. But Stephen wasn't just a waiter, and you're not just a soccer mom, or a mechanic, or a member of the quilting club.

You're a prophet. At least you can be, if you accept the opportunities the Lord opens up for you. This is one of the main points of Acts. Peter's first point in his first sermon tells us this:

> This is what was spoken by the prophet Joel:
> "In the last days, God says,
> I will pour out my Spirit on all people.
> Your sons and daughters will prophesy,
> your young men will see visions,
> your old men will dream dreams.

Even on my servants, both men and women,
I will pour out my Spirit in those days,
and they will prophesy." (Acts 2:16–18)

This point, in a patriarchal society, is huge. No longer does God's Spirit rest only on a select few. Now, through this new thing God is doing through Jesus, the Spirit empowers young men and old women, seventh-grade girls and sixty-year-old truck drivers. All of us can be God's servants. His prophets.

At the church where I preach, we have a senior saint named Ruth who goes to the jail every week and teaches people art. Because she hopes that if she gives them a healthier way to express themselves, they won't find themselves back in the vicious cycles that got them locked up.

She teaches art in the name of Jesus. Because God is on the side of justice, and our dear Ruth is on the side of God.

Another woman at our church, a woman named Susan, is a quiet, joyful servant who hates being in the spotlight. But every week you can find her at inner-city schools teaching at-risk kids how to read.

She knows what a difference this will make in their lives. God is on the side of justice, and Susan is on the side of God.

A couple of college students from our church named Jason and Steven have recently started going to some apartments across town to try to make a positive difference in the lives of some refugee children. Jason and Steven have started a soccer league for these kids who wouldn't be able to play otherwise.

Jason and Steven know God is on the side of justice, and they are on the side of God.

A woman named Linda was a flight attendant for thirty years. But she quit this job that she loved to start a non-profit agency called Eternal Threads. Linda now goes all over the world equipping girls whose only options to make money tend to be pretty dark. She teaches these young women how to make crafts to sell. She is giving them a way to eat that doesn't involve selling their souls.

God is on the side of justice, and Linda is on the side of God.

It is inevitable that if you do this kind of thing for long, eventually you'll bother people who don't understand. You may even have to speak against some things they like. But that goes with the territory, because you're a prophet.

God is calling all prophets, and in this sense we're all called to be prophets. Stephen's story is our story. This is the message of Acts. The resurrection can turn cowards into apostles, and waiters into prophets.

It did in Stephen's day. It still does.

A few years ago I heard the well-known preacher Tom Long tell the story of Flora Miller. Flora was a senior saint who lived during the heart of the civil rights movement in Atlanta. She was a white, third-grade Sunday school teacher in a conservative, all-white church.

At one point, the civil rights workers in Atlanta adopted the strategy of sending African-American Christians to white churches to force their hand on whether they would be as inclusive as the gospel requires. Flora's church found itself in a predicament. They knew their congregation might be "visited," so the leaders of the church met to decide what to do if someone of color showed up at their church.

One Sunday morning the leaders announced their decision. They stood up and told their people that, after much prayer, the elders of the church had decided that they would allow African-American guests to join the assembly "so long as space provides." They repeated that statement, slowly enunciating each word: "So long as space provides."

If you looked around that morning, you would have noticed that space was not an issue for this church. They met in a spacious building that could accommodate hundreds of other believers. This statement was not an earnest decision to stand against the racism of their day. It was a public relations stunt. It was a sham, a front.

Then they said it one more time, just in case anybody didn't understand the unspoken message. "They will be welcome, *so long as space provides.*"

That's when little old Flora Miller, who had been at that church most of her life and had served and loved these people for decades, girded her loins and stood up. Right in the middle of the elders' stinky announcement, this sweet, elderly, Sunday school teacher said, "Well, if we happen to run out of room, they can have my seat."[4]

To most folks she looked like just your average Sunday school teacher, but Flora Miller was a prophet standing against religious bigotry. Even though it was far from popular and even though it might have cost her valued friendships, she spoke truth.

The biblical word for that is "prophet." Stephen found out that choosing to be one may put you in a grave, but the resurrection assures us that prophets never die.

Chapter 5

King of
Kings

"The people who hanged Christ never, to do them justice, accused Him of being a bore—on the contrary; they thought Him too dynamic to be safe. It has been left for later generations to muffle up that shattering personality and surround Him with an atmosphere of tedium. We have very efficiently pared the claws of the Lion of Judah, certified Him 'meek and mild,' and recommended Him as a fitting household pet for pale curates and pious old ladies."

—Dorothy Sayers

One of the first things I learned about my wife when we were getting to know each other is that I was not her first boyfriend. Unlike me, she didn't have many problems getting people to be interested in her. In fact, after a few months of dating, I found out that my wife dated a guy named Josh Henderson in eighth grade.

Some of you might recognize that name. Josh was one of the stars in the movie *Step-Up*. He has been in several movies and television programs, and, as I write this, he is one of the main stars in the reboot of the television program *Dallas*.

If you were to google Josh Henderson, one of the first things that would show up is his picture without a shirt on. He's got muscles in places that most people don't even know exist. He's got washboard abs and huge biceps.

What can I say? Leslie has a type.

Worked into the DNA of our relationships is this idea of exclusivity. And when we talk about God, if we forget that God is a relational being, then we will miss a huge piece of the story the Scriptures are telling us.

And we will also think certain parts of the Bible are painting God as some kind of malevolent power in the sky. Because in the Scriptures God calls himself "a jealous God." And jealousy can sound really harsh if we ever forget that underneath it is a whole lot of love. But in God's case, just as in our romances, it's a love that refuses to share itself with any other competing allegiances.

This is one of the main plots of Scripture, that God is deeply involved in a story of winning back his people who have forgotten who is their true Lover.

It's a story that goes like this.

Competing Kingdoms

The book of 1 Kings starts off with King David on his deathbed. He's lived a long life and, overall, has been a great king, with a few left turns along the way. Even though he was involved in Bathsheba-gate, he will be remembered as Israel's best king.

But like the reigns of all human kings, this one has to come to an end, and that's where the problem starts. In most dynasties, the oldest son is expected to be next in line. But this isn't your ordinary kingdom, and David is not your ordinary king.

Instead of choosing Adonijah, his oldest son, David has chosen Solomon to be the heir to the throne. Crown prince Adonijah doesn't like this plan, so he plans a shady takeover. Adonijah sets up a coronation ceremony, complete with fifty chariot riders to go ahead of him. And he does all of this without informing David or Solomon. So when the news of this treachery leaks back to David, he starts planning a ceremony of his own. He tells Nathan the prophet to take Solomon to the center of town on a donkey. The prophet is instructed to anoint the new king with oil and seat him on the royal throne while proclaiming to all of Israel, "This is your true king."

And it works. Solomon becomes known throughout all Israel as the new king, and Adonijah is exposed as a parody.

Hang with me here; maybe you are thinking to yourself, "I thought I bought a book about Acts," but we will get there. First, though, one more stop in the story.

Noblemen and Kings

Herod Archelaus is a son of Herod the Great; but since the rulers of Palestine now derive their power and authority from Rome, they don't really have a dynasty. Each successor must be legitimized by Rome. So after Herod the Great dies, Archelaus (who had a hard enough time just to keep from being killed by his own paranoid father) has to travel to Rome to ask for his father's throne.

In other words, he leaves Jerusalem as a nobleman and returns as a king.

The local Jewish people aren't too happy to have another Herod reigning over them. The last years under Archelaus' demented old father have been a nightmare. So they send a delegation of diplomats to Rome to try to convince Caesar not to give Archelaus the throne.

That's how much they hate the new Herod.

In the light of this brief history lesson, hear a parable Jesus tells one day right before he enters Jerusalem. Notice how he tells the story.

> While they were listening to this, he went on to tell them a parable, because he was near Jerusalem and the people thought that the kingdom of God was going to appear at once. He said: "A man of noble birth went to a distant country to have himself appointed king and then to return. So he called ten of his servants and gave them ten minas. 'Put this money to work,' he said, 'until I come back.'
>
> "But his subjects hated him and sent a delegation after him to say, 'We don't want this man to be our king.' He was made king, however, and returned home." (Luke 19:11–15)

Instantly these people know who Jesus is talking about.

For some reason Jesus pauses before he enters Jerusalem and tells this story in a specific way, citing well-known events. For some reason, in his audience's minds, Jesus wants to conjure up Herod going to Rome and asking to be king.

Do you know what the next story is in Luke?

The Triumphal Entry

In the next story, Jesus is riding into Jerusalem on a donkey.

This seems so mild, but in reality what Jesus is doing here is the equivalent to riding into town on Air Force One. He is getting people to remember a specific time in their history—a time when there was another guy claiming to be king of Israel. This man sat on the throne but did not deserve to be there. And the real king stood up.

When he rides into town on this donkey, Jesus is footnoting a story they all know. He is telling the people of Israel, "Nobody who sits on this Jerusalem throne—none of the Herods or any of the Roman appointees who have replaced them—is your true king. I am the King of Israel."

Luke has good reasons for including in his Gospel these details of our Lord's Triumphal Entry into Jerusalem. Many people are still wondering who this strange Galilean is. His donkey ride into town gives them new information. Even the closest disciples of Jesus gain fresh insights into Jesus' true identity when they recall the words of Zechariah:

> Rejoice greatly, O Daughter of Zion!
>> Shout, Daughter of Jerusalem!
> See, your king comes to you,
>> righteous and having salvation,
>> gentle and riding on a donkey,
>> on a colt, the foal of a donkey. (Zech. 9:9)

For those in the Jerusalem streets who somehow fail to connect Zechariah's famous prophecy to the Galilean's choice of steeds that day, the Lord just keeps providing tips. Even the unpopular procurator Pontius Pilate will choose to advertise the truth about Jesus. He will be sarcastic in doing so, no doubt, but on the cross above the head of our Lord that ungodly man will post a sign that tells everybody on Golgotha, "This is the King of the Jews."

"Look at this man, bleeding in agony, dying as a common criminal," Pilate will tell the world. "This is your king."

Luke makes sure the readers of Part One of his story see this. And, of all the Gospel writers, he alone includes Jesus' blunt reply to Pilate's aggressive questioning.

"Are you the king of the Jews?" Pilate grills Christ.

Most of the time during his trial Jesus stands silent before his judges and accusers. "Like a sheep before its shearers is dumb, so he opened not his mouth," Isaiah predicted. Jesus has kept his mouth shut up until now.

But he answers Pilate.

"Yes," Jesus replies without hesitation, "it is as you say."

Only Luke, the Gospel writer who gives us the clearest picture of the ascension, also includes this clear, unequivocal answer of Jesus.

Israel has been waiting ever since David for the arrival of the often predicted King. God promised David that he would put one of his offspring on the throne. "I will establish the throne of his kingdom forever. I will be his father, and he will be my son" (2 Sam. 7:13–14).

Any neighbor of Jesus who is worth his salt can recite Isaiah's famous prediction that a child will be born, a son will be given, and this extraordinary child will be called "the Prince of Peace" and he will sit on David's throne (9:6–7).

Everybody in Jerusalem expects a Messiah. Some of them dream that this coming King will rid the Jewish nation of their oppressive Roman rulers. They can't wait for this promised King to show up. And when he finally does come, they miss him because they are looking for him in all the wrong places.

Their failure, like ours, is not the last word, however. Luke makes sure of that. His Gospel ends with Jesus on the way to heaven. His continuation of Jesus' story in Acts begins where he leaves off in the Gospel. Jesus is about to ascend to his Father.

Now let me pause here and say that at the heart of the Christian tradition is the cross and resurrection . . . and the ascension of Jesus. Some of us quickly embrace the crucifixion of Jesus and cherish the great sacrifice and solidarity that God shows through entering our suffering. And most Christians I know love to talk about the resurrection. But we don't talk much about the significance of Jesus' ascension.[1]

For some reason, we tend to brush the ascension aside. It appears to me that some of us even act like we are a bit embarrassed by the whole idea of Jesus ascending to heaven. Maybe it sounds a bit too much like an ancient version of Star Trek to take seriously.

But Luke knows exactly what he's doing . . . even if we don't.

The first readers of Luke's second book would have heard this story, not as science fiction, but as a claim to kingship. They knew that Augustus Caesar tried to prove his own heaven-endowed greatness by telling a tall tale about seeing Julius Caesar ascend to heaven as a comet during games being held in his honor.

If you were reading Luke's book back in the first or second century, when you read this part, you would have started looking over your shoulder, not unlike reading Karl Marx during the Red Scare.

Because the ascension isn't some church VBS-like story for us to help our children appreciate that Jesus can fly like Superman.

The point is that Jesus is now in heaven, in God's control booth, sitting at the right hand of God. The point is that Jesus, the still human, bodily resurrected Messiah, has now returned to heaven. God hasn't given up on his good creation. He's actually still a part of it. But now he reigns over it.

Perhaps this is why Peter mentions the ascension in his first sermon:

> Exalted to the right hand of God, [Jesus] has received from the Father the promised Holy Spirit and has poured out what you now see and hear. For David did not ascend to heaven, and yet he said, "The Lord said to my Lord: 'Sit at my right hand until I make your enemies a footstool for your feet.'" Therefore let all Israel be assured of this: God has made this Jesus, whom you crucified, both Lord and Messiah. (Acts 2:33–36)

Clearly, the ascension is central to the message of the early Christians. Because it is a picture, more than anything else, of the sovereignty of God.

C. S. Lewis used a metaphor to talk about the incarnation. He said that God had written himself into his own story. I like that image. Let me expand it by suggesting that the ascension is Jesus returning to being the author of the story.

He's now king of the universe.

And the rest of Acts treats us to story after story of the disciples going everywhere proclaiming that creation is under new management. Which does bring us finally to Acts 12.

The Real Lord

Later on in Luke, he tells us about one king, Herod Agrippa I, whose inflated ego turns out to be a fatal flaw:

> Then Herod went from Judea to Caesarea and stayed there. He had been quarreling with the people of Tyre and Sidon; they now joined together and sought an audience with him. After securing the support of Blastus, a trusted personal servant of the king, they asked for peace, because they depended on the king's country for their food supply.
>
> On the appointed day Herod, wearing his royal robes, sat on his throne and delivered a public address to the people. They shouted, "This is the voice of a god, not of a man." Immediately, because Herod did not give praise to God, an angel of the Lord struck him down, and he was eaten by worms and died.
>
> But the word of God continued to increase and spread. (Acts 12:19–24)

The first-century historian Josephus lets us know that Herod was wearing a special kind of clothing here. He had his tailors make him silver robes that were designed to reflect the sunlight, and then he would position himself in a place that would make him shine.

Kanye West, eat your heart out.

The goal of Herod's wardrobe was to make people think he was divine. But it's not just his clothes. All of Herod's life was oriented toward this. He wanted to be somebody he was not. He was trying to overstep his bounds. And now, just when all his political posturing and maneuvering were beginning to pay off, Herod got a taste of what Jesus' ascension really means—that Jesus is Lord and Herod is not.

Let's take this further . . . .

A few years ago as I was driving in Fort Worth, I saw a guy standing on the side of the road holding a sign that said in bright neon colors to all who passed by: "Repent or Burn."

Let me offer a couple of observations about this guy. To start with, I think I know what he was thinking. Would you believe that I have done this kind of thing before? That man probably genuinely cared about people, and I suspect that he really loved the Lord. He knew what the Scriptures say about judgment, and, like all loving Christians, he wanted as many people as possible to be spared that judgment.

Can you imagine doing what that man was doing? All day long? It's one thing to be shy about going up to people and telling them something like "God loves you and has a wonderful plan for your life." It's an entirely different thing to walk up to someone and say, "God is really, really ticked off at you."

To be honest, I don't like this evangelism method at all. I think it's not productive at best; and depending on the person, it can be arrogant and hateful. However, it does tap into a theme that runs throughout Scripture—the theme of judgment.

What the Bible says about it may be different than this guy thinks.

Caesar Isn't Lord

The Scriptures refer to God's final judgment repeatedly as "the day of the Lord." And, contrary to what you may have heard, in the first-century church people actually looked forward to it. It's not that these people all assumed that they were perfect or above judgment, but they did assume that their Creator God was good and full of grace.

And it was comforting to know that someone wise and just was keeping score.

In Romans 13, Paul tells the church to give honor and respect to the governing authorities, and rightfully so. God does not want society to disintegrate into chaos.

Think with me a moment about that text. Paul is writing to Jewish and Gentile Christians in Rome, where the slogan of the day is that Caesar is Lord. And while Paul does say we should give Caesar taxes, revenue, respect, and honor, he stops short of the main thing they were being commanded to give—worship. Caesar wanted people to worship him as the Lord; Herod Agrippa, whom we looked at earlier, wanted people to think he was divine. And the reason this was important to these men was that if Caesar was Lord, if Herod was Lord, there were no checks and balances to keep them accountable. They answered to no one.

Go back and read Romans 13 again in view of this and see if these thoughts don't shed some new light on it. Our presidents are powers ordained by God; our prime ministers and our kings, even our dictators, are powers ordained by God.

But they aren't God. There are presidents and kings, but there is only one King of kings.

The Bible's emphasis on judgment is not intended just to scare people, as some of us assume. Throughout the Old Testament, the prophets and psalmists welcomed God's judgment because they knew he would set right an unfair world. He would back the poor against the rich, the weak against the strong. When Mary sang her famous "Magnificat" after God told her that she would be the mother of the Messiah, this is exactly what she sang about. She praised God for judging fairly, for honoring a poor, powerless woman above those who enjoyed wealth and influence.

For thousands of years, the people of God have looked forward to and taken pleasure in serving a Lord who judges, and will judge, with love and mercy and equity.

A passage like Romans 13 is also a reminder to the powers that run this world that they answer to somebody greater than themselves. We often sing about Jesus as King of kings (as do the angels in heaven), but this title is more than just a good worship phrase. It's one of the deepest truths that the ascension of Jesus teaches us.

Our Lord in heaven rules over our systems and our governors, our kings and our presidents, our mayors and our preachers. And a day will come when all powers are brought fully under the feet of Jesus.

I wish that man in Fort Worth would put that on his sign.

There Can Only Be One

A few years ago when I was teaching in a jail ministry in Fort Worth, I was using some of the material that would later become this book. At one point, I wrote a sermon on the ascension called "How to Start a Riot." I got a call from the jail chaplain the next week. For some reason he thought that passing out stuff that said "How to Start a Riot" might not be the wisest decision for a jail ministry!

But I wonder. If the people who administer our prisons knew what is really in the book of Acts, would they let it be read in there either?

The Bible is illegal in many countries. Could it be that those countries know something about the book that we have forgotten— that underneath our Precious Moments memorabilia and inside our leather-bound Bibles we hold the most revolutionary story the world has ever known?

Do you know what the word *Christian* actually means? It means people of the king. And we get this term from Acts.

This means that if you are a Christian, then you have more in common with your Christian brothers and sisters who are being persecuted on the opposite side of the world than you do with your next-door neighbor who is just like you in so many ways but is not a Christian.

You serve the King.

Look at what the earliest Christians were actually accused of:

> The Jews became jealous, and with the help of some ruffians in the marketplaces they formed a mob and set the city in an uproar. While they were searching for Paul and Silas to bring them out to the assembly, they attacked Jason's house. When they could not find them, they dragged Jason and some believers before the city authorities, shouting, "These people who have been turning the world upside down have come here also, and Jason has entertained them as guests. They are all acting contrary to the decrees of the emperor, saying that there is another king named Jesus." (Acts 17:5–7 NRSV)

They were turning the world upside down, all because they preached that Jesus was king.

People in the first-century world knew something that more modern readers tend to forget: there can be only one king. If Jesus is king, then there is no other. This might be why Revelation ends with everyone laying down their crowns; because when you finally see God, you realize the right to wear a diadem was always his.

Many years ago, Voltaire said he was sure that Christianity would die within fifty years. A few years later, they buried Voltaire in a church, and the way of Jesus is still going. Hitler claimed to be the one who would save the world, and today a Bible translation center is housed in what used to be his headquarters.

Whether it was Herod's Caesar, the ancient Jewish leaders, or more recent people like Hitler or Stalin, everyone in power seems to be trying to stop this Jesus movement. But for all their trying, they can't.

"The word of God continued to increase and spread" (Acts 12:24).

Jesus, the sovereign Lord, stands both with us and above us, drawing all things back to himself. Because he is the King of kings.

This may go against the grain of many modern readers' sensibilities. We like our gods to be less demanding, relegated to certain buildings for certain hours of the week. We like to think that if we show up, do some prescribed rituals like singing and praying, then God will somehow be obligated to keep sharing his throne.

That's one of the most Western messages there is—it's anti-gospel.

Did you ever wonder why the people in Acts were always filled with joy, even in the worst circumstances? They would get arrested and beaten, imprisoned and even murdered, and they were still singing and praising the Lord for whom they suffered. Joy was central to the first Christians' lives, even though by all appearances they should have been miserable.

I think this was true because they had grasped a basic part of the ultimate reality: that there is only one God, and none of us are him.

This may be one reason we live in a culture where anxiety medication is the number one prescription drug. When the world centers around you, you have more than enough to worry about.

Christian history overflows with the stories of brave men and women who have died refusing to bend their knee to another king. This unbending faith, this unflinching allegiance helps to explain why the earliest Christians were filled with such joy. They knew who the king was.

All of us can find real relief in recognizing that we don't run the universe. Knowing that your well-being doesn't depend on who's on the throne or in office, or on whether or not some bill gets passed can also remove a load of anxiety.

All of us can find genuine relief in trusting that God is in charge and he is good. Because those first Christians knew who was running the universe and that he knew them, they could hold their heads high on the toughest days. Because they followed a God who had defeated death and was Lord of everything, they knew that nothing could separate them from his love.

Today we are so far removed from Christ's ascension that hearing about it or thinking about it fails to light a fire in our hearts. Not so in the days of Acts, right after Jesus went to heaven and the church began.

Remember the picture Luke gives us of Stephen, the fellow who tried to tell a crowd about the risen, ascended Lord? The more he told them, the madder they got. As Stephen talked to them about Jesus, they became ballistic. "When they heard this," Luke tells us, "they were furious and gnashed their teeth at him."

Then notice what really set off this angry mob. "Stephen, full of the Holy Spirit, looked up to heaven and saw the glory of God, and Jesus standing at the right hand of God. 'Look,' he said, 'I see heaven open and the Son of Man standing at the right hand of God.'"

Stephen bore witness to the reality of Jesus' ascension and his position of honor beside God on the throne. And look how that crowd reacted: "At this they covered their ears and, yelling at the top of their voices, they all rushed at him, dragged him out of the city and began to stone him" (Acts 7:54–58).

Stephen's vision of the ascended Lord set off that mob. It's also what can give a Christian a window of peace in the middle of any storm. Jesus stands both with us, and over us. He's the King of the Universe and all of history answers to him.

Chapter 6

Church
Is a Verb

"To go into church is great, but to go out and put it all into action, that's where it all is at."

    —Johnny Cash[1]

"A Church which pitches its tents without constantly looking out for new horizons, which does not continually strike camp, is being untrue to its calling. . . . [We must] play down our longing for certainty, accept what is risky, live by improvisation and experiment."

    —Hans Kung[2]

In Luke's Gospel he tells us of a time when Jesus is talking to a group of religious people and they have challenged him on a couple of points.

They don't like Jesus' teaching on money. These critics actually start sneering at Jesus, so he decides to tell them a story about a rich man who is dressed in purple and has the latest fashions and lives in luxury. And then Jesus tells them that outside this man's mansion, outside his gate, is a beggar named Lazarus, who longed to eat what fell from the rich man's table. It's an incredibly heart-wrenching story—at one point dogs even begin to lick the poor man's sores;

but the most intriguing part of Jesus' story is how he introduces the characters.

In Jesus' story, one character is named, the other is described. We meet the beggar Lazarus, but it's like the rich man isn't fully human; he doesn't even have a name. Which seems odd when you think about it, because this isn't how our world works.

The world does it the opposite way. The street people don't have names. The rich and prestigious we tend to honor and pay attention to, so Bill Gates, Donald Trump, and Mark Zuckerburg are household names. Meanwhile some people in my congregation still know me as "the new preacher."

The Bible loves to do this. The book of Exodus begins by introducing us to the Pharaoh, the most powerful person in the world, but Exodus doesn't even give us his name. Then in the same chapter, we are told the names of the two midwives who save some Jewish babies.

The Bible loves to turn the world upside down. This scriptural style for storytelling is like saying once upon a time there was Steve the janitor, and there was a guy who owned Microsoft.

Obviously, God has a different perspective on society than we do. So Jesus tells us in his story that the rich man has a gate.

I've been to lots of places in the world, and every society I've seen has managed to create some form of gated communities. This is an arrangement that serves a purpose. Gates keep people out. A gate insulates people from those that they don't want around them. Gates do their job well.

It's important to know that when Jesus says that Lazarus longed to eat what the rich man ate. This probably implies more than a desire for food. To eat with someone often implies something deeper than just eating. It's about community. Lazarus desperately needs food, but, just as pressing, he needs a friend.

But the rich man doesn't have to interact with Lazarus. He's safe in his home. Inside that gate the rich man never has to see poor Lazarus' sores. He never sees the gauntness of the beggar's malnourished body. In fact, he rarely sees much of anything going on outside his sheltered, pampered world.

Gates keep people out—but they also keep people in.

The Future Today

After Jesus brilliantly captures the relationship of these two now-famous characters in just a few sentences, he shifts the scene to give us another look at them.

Inevitably, both the rich man and the beggar die, and one goes to Torment and the other to Paradise. The word *torment* here is the same word that was used to describe the process for testing coins. That's what is going on here. Just as the intense fire melted alloys that might have been used to corrupt and cheapen coins, so the flames of Torment expose the errors in the rich man's life and the dross in his soul.

Jesus also tells us that Lazarus was "in the bosom of Abraham." Our modern Bible translations simplify this by telling us that the starving beggar is now dining in heaven alongside none other than Abraham.

In Jesus' time, when people ate, they lay on couches instead of sitting in chairs around the table. This sounds like such a stress-free way to eat. Which I think raises the question: why don't we do this anymore?

Eating like this was quite comfortable and convenient . . . almost lazy. Unless you want to talk to the person on your left side. To speak to them face to face, you have to interrupt the dining process long enough to swap elbows in order to face that person. You have to do this *unless* that person is an intimate friend or close relative. Then, instead of changing elbows, you can just lay your head back onto the chest of that person and speak to them within inches of their face. This is what our older Bibles are describing when they say that someone like Lazarus is "reclining in the bosom" of another person.

Not only does Lazarus now have food. Not only has he landed on the right side of the Paradise/Torment gulf. He now has a close friend.

And the rich man is now in Torment. He is now alone and isolated.

Both men got their wish. What they wanted most on earth was granted to them in the next life as well. In Jesus' story, death exposes what both people had been chasing all along.

The rich man sees Lazarus afar off and doesn't even talk to him; he talks to Abraham. He wants Abraham to dispatch Lazarus on an errand. "Have him bring me water." He still sees Lazarus as a servant, as somehow inferior to him.

The next thing he asks for is that Lazarus go warn his five living brothers about this horrible place. Which sounds noble, until you realize that this guy still sees Lazarus as his messenger. He still is treating Lazarus like a slave.

Clarence Jordan, the well-known African-American pastor, said about this story, "Lazarus ain't going to run no mo of your errands, rich man." The problem is that the selfishness of the rich man won't die. He is in hell, because hell is still in him.

Let me say that this is not a parable against rich people. Don't overlook the fact that Abraham is a main character in this story, and he was one of the richest people in the Bible.

Jesus does not tell this story to condemn the rich. He tells it to warn us about using wealth to insulate ourselves from the very people God wants us to use our resources to help.

This is a parable about waking up to right now. Jesus is teaching truth about what is going on in God's reality at this moment. That's what the thirsty rich man wants his five surviving brothers to know, that this is the reality of God that is happening right now.

This story is not just about the rich man and Lazarus. It's also about the five brothers.

In one sense, the rich man gets his wish. He wants his story told to those who are still living. That's exactly what Jesus is doing, but the story ends before Luke can tell us how they took it. The lights go out on the story before we know what those brothers did with this truth. Jesus leaves this question unresolved. If this was a movie, this unresolved ending would haunt us. We're left wondering, is this story a dream or not? But Jesus knows exactly what he's doing.

Because we are those brothers.

In effect, Jesus is asking, "Does this vision of the life to come change the way you are living now?"

The Gates We Build

But let's take this a bit further. What happens when our approach to gates becomes a system? What if it's not just one person but a whole group of people who get shut out? What kind of evil have we invented when we learn how to systematize ways to keep some people in and some people out?

Those questions bring us back to the book of Acts.

One day Peter and John were going up to the temple at the time of prayer—at three in the afternoon. Now a man crippled from birth was being carried to the temple gate called Beautiful, where he was put every day to beg from those going into the temple courts. When he saw Peter and John about to enter, he asked them for money. Peter looked straight at him, as did John. Then Peter said, "Look at us!" So the man gave them his attention, expecting to get something from them. (Acts 3:1–5)

They laid this poor man at the gate, Luke tells us. Everybody else is going into the Temple, but not this guy. He knows the prohibitions; cripples aren't allowed inside the holy Temple. But they can beg outside the gate.

So he waits there for somebody to show him some pity and toss him a coin or two. This is one of the busiest times of the day, a good time to beg. He's there mainly to get some shekels for food. But his more urgent need is not his hunger for food, it's hunger for community. He desperately needs someone to notice that he exists.

I think we all know what it's like to walk past a person who is begging.

Maybe it's because we have been burned by people who abused our generosity. But over time, we develop defenses; we learn to view the world in a certain way that can keep us from even seeing people in need. We come up with lots of reasons to ignore them.

Back in Luke's day plenty of people would have been quick to say that this man is lame because of his sin or his parents' sin. In other words, he deserves to be crippled and poor. But that doesn't work for Peter and John. In their eyes this man isn't just some theological argument. He's a person.

That's why these men don't just give something to the beggar. They ask him to look at them. Luke is really big on what we see. It's in Luke's Gospel that Jesus asks Simon the Pharisee if he sees the sinful woman in front of him (7:44). It's in his Gospel that the disciples' eyes are opened (24:31), and he tells us in Acts that Saul's blinded eyes are opened (9:18).

That's what's going on here. The apostles want this lame man to see them. They want him to know that they see him too.

The disciples don't give a handout; instead they tell the man that they don't have silver and gold, but they've got something better. Life. And with a word, that's exactly what they give him. The man stands up and starts walking for the first time ever. And he goes into the Temple, probably for the first time in his life. By the end of this, the (formerly) lame man is jumping and leaping in the Temple.

What a great picture! It's an incredible story of joy and inclusion and restoration. Like the prodigal coming home, this man is about to party. And, let's be honest, he's got a great reason to dance.

All of his life he's been viewed as second class. He's used to sitting outside the gate. Now suddenly he's able to go through it. And, when a crowd gathers to watch this lame man dance, Peter steps up and preaches his second sermon in Acts.

Peter makes it clear that this healing miracle is not something that he and John have done on their own. This crippled man is now walking and leaping on two strong legs in the name and by the power of Jesus of Nazareth. These religious leaders who run the Temple were so desperate to remain in control that they killed Jesus just a few weeks earlier. But God rewrote the ending to this story when he raised Jesus from the grave.

Fearlessly Peter points a finger at the very people who were responsible for Jesus' arrest and crucifixion. But in his sermon, he makes it clear that this story of Jesus is not some tragic ending; it's what the Scriptures had been pointing to all along.

Opening All the Gates

Listen to Peter here as he brings the story of Jesus into conversation with several different Old Testament stories. He's letting them know that from Abraham to Samuel to Moses this story is as old as the world itself.

> When Peter saw this, he said to them: "Men of Israel, why does this surprise you? Why do you stare at us as if by our own power or godliness we had made this man walk? The God of Abraham, Isaac and Jacob, the God of our fathers, has glorified his servant Jesus. You handed him over to be killed, and you disowned him before Pilate, though he had decided to let him go." (Acts 3:12–13)

Peter knows exactly what he's doing. He quotes here directly from Exodus 3, which is the story of God showing up to talk to Moses in a burning bush. Peter is quoting one of the most famous stories in the history of Israel, a story of the time when God delivered his people from slavery.

I think it's amazing that God started the whole Exodus story with a shrub. The epic story of Israel and God began with a tiny bush on fire. This is a story that reminds us that God can show up anywhere.

This lame man being healed, this demonstration of new power, happens *outside the Temple*. God is on the move, and if the religious institutions are not, then they will miss out on what God is about to do to redeem his world. In the rest of the chapter Peter explains to church people that God won't limit his activities to the space inside their gates.

The people do not come to the Temple that day expecting to see a miracle. They are used to hearing stories about miracles but not to seeing one walking around right in front of them.

That's part of the message of Acts 3.

But there's another reason, I think, that Peter quotes the Moses story on this occasion. It's because God is about to do something similar to what Moses did. In Jesus, God is starting a new Exodus. Once more the people of God will be delivered from the slavery of death. What God did in the resurrection is going to change every part of the world. Even death will one day give back what it owes.

God didn't cause this man at the Temple gate to be born lame. It was never his intention for the world to be like this.

And that's why Peter turns around and tells the shocked crowd this:

> Repent, then, and turn to God, so that your sins may be
> wiped out, that times of refreshing may come from the
> Lord, and that he may send the Christ, who has been
> appointed for you—even Jesus. He must remain in heaven
> until the time comes for God to restore everything, as
> he promised long ago through his holy prophets. (Acts
> 3:19–21)

The thrust of this story, and every miraculous story in Acts, is never about the miracle. Peter's point is not, "See, this kind of thing still happens!" Peter's point is not the restoration of the man; it is what the restoration of the man is pointing toward.

Letting this lame man walk again is really cool, but you haven't seen anything yet. One day God is going to do for the world what we saw happen to this man. This is just a preview of coming attractions.

I've sat at the foot of hospital beds and prayed for God to heal people I love, only to deliver the eulogy later that week. I've seen entire churches on their knees praying for God to heal someone . . . and it didn't happen.

I've preached dozens of the funerals of infants or spouses and dear friends, all who had people praying for healing, but didn't get it. If you've got any kind of heart at all, there will be times when you will find yourself disappointed with God.

I believe that God is at work in the world, but I also have learned this doesn't mean God works the way I think he should.

God isn't about just healing cancer every now and then. God is not about just delivering people from addictions occasionally. God is not about just performing a rare, occasional miracle so that everyone can oooh and aaaah.

This healing is a sign for us, an arrow pointing to a time when things won't be this way anymore.

When there will be no more cancer.

No more suffering. No more death.

Through Jesus God is restoring all the things broken in the Fall. On this day at the Temple, the Lord opens the gate and restores this man to the community that had shut him out.

What's great about this story is how it ends. Peter and John walk with this guy into the Temple. Right past the gate.

This beggar needed more than crumbs. He needs community. The people who have been seeing him day by day outside the gate now are forced to see him not just as a theological dilemma or an economic drain. Now they see him as a person.

Remember how Jesus ends his parable of the Rich Man and Lazarus? At the end of that story a great gulf separates them. The rich man had spent his life wanting distance from those who needed him, and when he died, his wishes were granted.

That's a scary thought: that God may give us what we want.

I think we have to be extremely careful about categorizing the world into "us and them," of building walls and gates, because there's a good chance, whenever we put one up, we'll find Jesus on the other side of it.

One of Luke's favorite metaphors for this band of believers was "the Way." Now by the power of Jesus this man is walking. This is a story of movement. It's a story of people who realize that God is on the move.

There is a phrase I hear from time to time that drives me crazy. I'll hear people talking about finding a church home, and then they'll say something like, "We're church shopping." And that makes me want to go home and kick my dog.

Shopping for churches is like playing Legos with uranium. Maybe that's one of the reasons why so many churches have become seen as little more than domesticated bits of American suburbia.

Because, let's face it, if this whole thing is about just coming and sitting in a pew, writing a check, singing a song, and listening to some person talk . . . if that's all this is, then you can call it what you want. But let's not call it church.

Church isn't some gated community. Church is a verb.

Luke's Gospel opens and closes at the Temple; this is a really big deal for him. Because he knows what the Temple is and will one day be. In Isaiah, God promised that one day the Temple will be big enough for the whole world to worship in. Because one day, the whole world will be the Temple of God.

Just as his glory filled the ancient Temple, in the end God's glory will fill all the universe, and he will welcome people from every tribe and tongue and nation. Everyone will be invited. The lame, the sick, the rich, the poor, female and male, Jews and Gentiles, Democrats and Republicans—God is creating a new humanity in Jesus.

Church matters, not because it is the only place we can meet God, but because it is where we learn to meet God everywhere else. Church is where we learn how to see God in the people who are outside the walls. Church is where we learn that God is on the move. That Jesus is The Way.

Chapter 7

Not for Sale

"In Consumer Christianity, our concern is not primarily whether people are transformed to reflect the countercultural values of God's Kingdom, but whether they are satisfied."
— Skye Jethani

"Have it your way."
— Burger King

Before Jesus starts his ministry, before he works a single miracle or preaches his first sermon, he goes on quite possibly the world's worst vacation.

He goes out into the desert to fast for forty days. And Luke tells us that "he was hungry." Thank you, Luke, for clearing that up for us. Forty days without a bite to eat and he was hungry! Luke evidently went to the school of redundancy.

But what is happening here during these desert days is pretty incredible.

Matthew, Mark, and Luke all begin their Gospels by telling how Jesus starts his ministry. Things are just beginning to pick up some steam in the Gospels, and then all three Gospels stop us and make sure we pay attention to this interlude.

Jesus is baptized in the Jordan, and he goes out into the wilderness for forty days.

Which is significant.

Do you realize that to get there, he passes through the same water Israel passed through when they were being delivered? And that he also goes out to wander in the same wilderness they traversed?

You probably know this story. Satan tempts Jesus three different times, and all three times Jesus responds from the book of Deuteronomy. A book that, by the way, came out of Israel's time in that wilderness.

One thing the Gospel writers are showing us here is that this is what a real Israelite looks like. What a real human looks like. Jesus is what it looks like to be the people of God. Where those Exodus Israelites failed, Jesus is going to show us how to succeed.

But I think it's important to pay attention to the way Satan tempts Jesus. If this is what the devil came after Jesus with, is it possible that he would come after Jesus' followers with the same stuff? "The devil said to him, 'If you are the Son of God, tell this stone to become bread.' Jesus answered, 'It is written: 'Man does not live on bread alone'" (Luke 4:3–4).

Since Jesus has been fasting for forty days, this probably seems like a pretty decent idea. Jesus has needs, and Satan proposes a plan for him to have them met. The temptation here is to turn the stuff of creation into something useful. I like the way Eugene Peterson talks about this temptation in our lives today:

> The devil wants us to do the same: Follow Jesus but then use Jesus to fulfill needs. First our own and then the needs of all the hungry people around us. This is the temptation

to deal with myself and others first and foremost as consumers. It is the temptation to define life in consumer terms
and then devise plans and programs to accomplish them in
Jesus' name.[1]

But what if the gospel isn't like that? What if it's got different purposes for our lives than what we've been taught to expect from it?

Now I think that's a fine way to approach a soccer league, or a
gym membership, or our participation in the vitamin-of-the-month
club. But too often that kind of thinking is the grid through which
we view the rest of life.

Sometimes it's how we approach God, or faith, or church. If we
do approach church that way, either we must stop or we must stop
calling it church.

In our culture the way we are starting to view being the people
of God sounds little like the way the first Christians talked and a lot
like the people who went against the gospel.

Let me explain.

Simon Says

The first time Luke tells us about any Christian preacher setting foot
outside of the Jewish cul de sac of Jerusalem and Judea is after the
first Christians had been persecuted. They are running for their lives
and preaching about the Kingdom of God whenever they go. One of
them, a man named Philip, heals people along the way and casts out
demons, and Luke tells us that Philip is doing all of this in Samaria.

For most of us that sounds incidental, but in the day it was written this is a huge deal for Philip even to be in Samaria.

Samaritans were the most detestable people for orthodox Jews.
They were the mixed breeds. They had intermarried with people from
other nations, so pure Jews didn't have a lot of tolerance for Samaritans.

But Samaritans are a really big deal for Luke. Maybe because he himself is not a Jew and he's had some experience with how that feels when you have to be around zealous Jews.

In the New Testament outside of Luke's writing, Samaritans are mentioned just four times. Luke mentions them a dozen times. Luke is making sure we remember that the gospel reconciles us not just to God but also to each other.

You and I can play the prodigal's older brother if we want to. We can pout and sulk about the inclusiveness of God's grace. But if we do, we ourselves just might miss out on God's reconciling love.

Like Simon.

When Simon first steps onto the pages of Acts, we find out that he is a sorcerer, and a pretty good one. He has amazed all of the people of Samaria, and "had told everyone that he was someone great." Obviously we don't have to do that today; that's why someone invented business cards.

But when Simon sees all the ways that God is working, he wants in. Simon becomes one of the first sorcerers to become a part of the Jesus movement. He believes the good news about Jesus the King and is baptized. But that's not enough for Simon. He starts to stalk Philip. Acts says he follows him everywhere. And Simon notices that some of the other new Christians seem to be getting a better deal than he did. Peter and John had rolled into town and now they are laying hands on some people and praying for them to receive the gift of the Holy Spirit. And here is where Simon makes his crucial mistake:

> When Simon saw that the Spirit was given at the laying on of the apostles' hands, he offered them money and said, "Give me also this ability so that everyone on whom I lay my hands may receive the Holy Spirit."

Peter answered: "May your money perish with you, because you thought you could buy the gift of God with money! You have no part or share in this ministry, because your heart is not right before God. Repent of this wickedness and pray to the Lord. Perhaps he will forgive you for having such a thought in your heart. For I see that you are full of bitterness and captive to sin."

Then Simon answered, "Pray to the Lord for me so that nothing you have said may happen to me." (Acts 8:18–24)

When Luke says Simon was a magician, we should not immediately jump to scenes from our sixth-grade birthday party or "Arrested Development." Luke talks about magic often in Acts, and he's always pretty hard on it. Not because Luke is trying to pick a fight with all the Harry Potter fans, but because he knows what this kind of magic is about.

Back in Luke's day, a magician was a person who claimed he could control the gods or powers by various arts of sorcery. Some people, for example, wore charms that said, "To Athena, the goddess of love." They might wear such a charm in order to win the goddess' favor so that the girl down the street would love them. Or sometimes they would follow superstitions such as eating garlic and onions to get a certain girl to love them (which seems counterproductive).

Everyone knew the gods were the forces that were out there, and you could persuade them to do what you wanted—you could get your way. If you knew how to barter with them.

Simon is a magician, a sorcerer, which means this is how he makes his living.

When he offers Peter money, we immediately know where this money is coming from. He gets the gods to do things for him.

I know this sounds primitive, but is our world really different?

A few years ago, after dropping a potentially game winning pass, one NFL wide receiver ranted to God on Twitter, "I praise you 24/7!!! And this is how you do me!!! You expect me to learn from this??? How??? I'll never forget this!! Ever!!"[2]

For him, worship and church attendance were a means to an end. A way to get God to act on his behalf. His approach to God was, in a word, magic.

Magic is a method of defense against forces we are helpless against. It was most common among the poor and the people who didn't have power socially and politically. Magic was their way of grasping for help. And if you don't get this yet, then just stick around. Wait until you find out that someone you love has been told, "It's cancer," or, "It's terminal."

It's not just our health. Most of us don't live in fear of when the next tornado or hurricane is coming our way. We have meteorologists to tell us. This is what Simon does in his day. Simon has a business. He makes his living by selling control to people who need it badly. His marketing is shock and awe, and now someone has trumped him. And Simon wants in on the winning side.

Simon approaches the gospel asking, "What can I get out of it?"

One of the symptoms of Simon's view of God is how he tries to relate to him. Simon tries to buy God. He tries to turn God into some kind of divine commodity. Which is a problem we Christians have struggled with all our days.

A professor of sociology at Notre Dame recently coined a phrase that I think is spot on. He says that the main religion of the Western world today is Moralistic Therapeutic Deism. What that means is that God serves as a combination of a divine judge, butler, and therapist.[3]

There's this idea that God is distant and removed from our day-to-day reality, but every now and then this God will reach in to fix some of our problems. God exists to meet our needs or to make us feel better about ourselves. Let me confess that I get this concept of God. I think it's pretty understandable that our culture thinks this way about him. After all, we think about everything else in these terms.

We are accosted on a daily basis by advertisements that tell us we are at the center of the universe. Did you know that on any given day you see or hear somewhere around 3,500 desire-inducing advertisements? And we can't pretend as if they don't have a significant amount of influence on our desires and ideas about what it means to be human. Companies spend billions of dollars in marketing to us for a good reason. It works.

Did you know there was never a mention of bad breath in popular culture until the invention of Listerine?[1] Our culture has been shaped, we are shaped, in large part by what we are taught to want and consume.

Homo Economicus

A while ago I read the memoir of a woman who committed not to buy anything for a year. She and her husband thought this would be a pretty simple life experiment. What they didn't see coming is how much of their identity was tied to buying things. Her observation was that we don't just consume; we have become consumers. Here's her way of talking about this:

> If you ask a Neoclassical capitalist economist, the free market is the epitome of Intelligent Design. Inside this rational system, claim these economists, the consumer—Homo Economicus—is also rational. He is well-informed and good at balancing his current needs and desires against those in the long term and then deciding where to put his money.

> Homo Economicus is abstracted from the society; he is not exactly a person, but a consumer, and as such, he is motivated by one thing, self-interest.[5]

I would argue that when we think of ourselves primarily as consumers, it becomes really hard to understand the gospel. Because the Scripture is crystal clear that the way we feel about God is deeply connected to how we treat the people around us.

We have learned to personify our objects and objectify our people. Remember those brilliant Apple TV ads? They started off with a nerdy looking guy saying, "I'm a PC," and the cooler, trendy guy saying, "I'm a Mac." I thought those ads were brilliant, but they also came with the baggage of some toxic ideas. No object is as important as the persons next to us.

But I'm not sure we really believe that anymore.

No wonder our culture has found it easier to walk away from marriage or from any of our relationships, including church. When we think of relationships in consumer terms, then the question we ask is, "What do I get out of it?"

Community doesn't work like that.

Henri Nouwen once said, "Community is the place where the person who you least want to be around just happens to live."

I'm a B.U.I.C.K, a Brought-Up-In-Church-Kid. I've spent my entire life deeply tied into a community of faith, both as a member and, for the past decade, as a minister. And I know us. Time and time again I've seen people leave a church because they didn't like the programs or the people, or because somebody said something hurtful.

We leave churches because churches have people. And we've been taught that our individual preference is more important than the community.

Any church you go to is going to have people who require extra grace, and in any church you go to, chances are you are going to be someone else's person who requires extra grace. Instead of viewing this as a problem, we might ask, "What if God is trying to work on my sharp edges or to help someone else with theirs?"

When iron sharpens iron, there's always friction. But there is a deeper issue to this than just how we look at people.

Churches and Cruise Ships[6]

Back in the 1800s the primary way immigrants came to the US was on big ships. They would sail into New York Harbor, straining for a glance of the Statue of Liberty, a symbol of a better life.

There wasn't a lot of competition between the ships because they had more than enough business to go around. Until one day the first passenger plane flew and overnight turned the Atlantic Ocean into "The Pond."

Soon the ships were retired to rust in the docks.

That is, until some enterprising people started to realize that they could revamp these ships, put some theaters in them, include a swimming pool or two, and call their voyages cruises. The goal was no longer to get people from point A to point B, but to cram as many entertainment options as possible onto the ship.

The ship was no longer the means, it had become the destination. Just like some churches.

If a church's mission is just bringing people into the building, then its vision is too small. For the church of Jesus, the goal is never just membership; it is discipleship.

Do you know what's interesting about this story of Simon?

In Acts 6, just a couple of chapters earlier, the Christian leaders had a problem. Some of the Grecian Christian widows were getting overlooked in the food distribution, so the Greek members were starting to complain. But Luke uses an interesting word to describe their complaining. He uses the exact same word that the book of Exodus uses for the Israelites' complaining in the wilderness.

It wasn't just that they wanted the widows fed. It wasn't the widows complaining. It was the Greek Christians, and the problem was that they wanted someone else to feed them. As if the church is a place where you can go for religious goods and services.

Those complainers had forgotten that they were the church.

And tucked between the story of Simon trying to buy God's gift and the Grecian Jews complaining, we find chapter seven, a story about the first Christian martyr.

Think about the book of Acts from a consumer perspective for a second. What would the sales pitch to join this movement look like?

Anybody looking to die a horrible death? Would anyone like to live in constant danger of being beheaded? If so, then have we ever got the thing for you!

I often hear people say that they left their old church because they were looking for more. I'm sure that people leave the church I serve because they are looking for more. Maybe sometimes that is justified. But I would caution you about looking for a church that just makes you feel comfortable but doesn't mention that the call of God is to die to yourself.

Consumer Christianity is diametrically opposed to what following Jesus is all about. The problem with trying to make a commodity out of God is that he's not a product. He's wild and untamable and can't be controlled or manipulated.

One problem with making the church a commodity is that the things we need the most are things we won't always want. If we enter church with a kind of stockholder mentality, then the scary truth is that you might eventually find a church that never makes you uncomfortable.

They might have every program you want. But they might never cause you to look more like Jesus.

I hear some teachers say that if you will just believe in Jesus, then your finances will be better, you won't deal with depression, and your teeth will be whiter. But I know a lot of broke, depressed Christians with brown teeth.

That's what is so damaging about any kind of prosperity gospel. It's what is so dangerous about approaching God or the church as a product. It implies that God somehow views the world the way we've been taught to.

A lot of times when I hear people talk about God, I think to myself that I signed up for a revolution and what I am hearing sounds more like a home-shopping network.

It sounds a lot like what Luke calls magic.

Some Christians get pretty worked up over the Harry Potter books, without realizing the irony that the biblical idea of magic is a lot more like the way we approach God than stories about teens at Hogwarts.

Magic is trying to leverage or control God to do what you want him to do. Legalism (performing rituals that we think God is obligated to honor) is the magic a lot of us have tried to perform during the past fifty years.

Today, we don't call it magic; we call it consumerism.

The gospel has been reduced to a transaction: give an hour a week, ten percent of your income, and you're cool. If that's all it is, then we can call it something else, but let's not call it church.

Do you realize what's happening here in Acts?

These two groups of people—Jews and Samaritans, people who have been estranged for centuries, people who hate one another with a passion—are being brought together by the gospel. People who were crippled are walking again!

And Simon is missing it.

Everyone else is filled with joy; they're caught up in what God is doing.

But not Simon. He's asking the question, What's in it for me? Simon wants to use Jesus for his own gain, but I want to ask him, Is there anything better, Simon? What more could you want? I think that's what Luke is asking us. What more could you want than this?

The church is the only community in the world where the question, "What's in it for me?" just doesn't make sense. The power of God is not for sale.

When you decided to follow Jesus, you joined a movement of God's redemptive history. God is in the business of reconciling all things in a broken world back to himself. He's piecing back the world one molecule at a time. And you get to be a part of it.

Racism, cancer, death, and a host of similar curses will be no longer. The old order of things is passing away, and we get to join in with the living God in this grand undertaking to make the world new again.

Put a price tag on that.

Chapter 8

Weak Is the **New Strong**

*"He is the King of kings largely because He lets himself get beat up.
He is victorious not despite His scars, but because of them."*
—Jonathan Martin[1]

A few years ago, a friend and I were working out at our local gym. We had finished for the day and were in the locker room changing when we saw this mountain of a man hovering over us. This guy was huge. He would show up on some radars. And the first words this giant said to us were, "Do we have a problem?"

Now if you know me, you know that I am not a very big person. I'm five-foot-seven and my body type oscillates somewhere between out-of-shape and husky. So the idea that my friend and I would pick a problem with Captain Cranky over here is laughable, but he wasn't laughing.

Then we saw it. Apparently, the bench we had chosen to put our gym bags on was the same bench he had chosen. Now his bag was on the floor, and our bags were right where his had just been. I blame my friend.

Captain Cranky said, "Would you like to take this outside?"

And we said, "We don't see what good could possibly come of that."

We apologized profusely and then tucked our tails and ran away. It wasn't until we were out in the parking lot that our survival instincts started to die down and our male egos started to kick in. We started talking about what we should have said. We should have told him that we didn't think he needed a bag to carry, since all the steroids were already in his system. Or that perhaps he solved problems like a caveman, but we were too professional to stoop to his level.

We thought about going back to settle the score with our wit. But then I decided that would just be stooping to his level. It would be petty to try to get revenge.

I'll just write about it in a book.

Since the Fall, this has been the way the world has worked. Might makes right. Only the strong survive. And to be honest, it makes sense. It is, after all, the most efficient way to run the world. And it is the world that Jesus was born into.

When Strength Is Weak

This is the system that is firmly in place when the earliest Christians start preaching about Jesus. This poses a problem. They are just a fledgling group of peasants and slaves. They don't have much going for them. If we were reading this story for the first time, we would expect that this would be the end of them.

What is fascinating to me about those earliest Christians, however, is how they responded to the challenge. We read time and time again from Scripture and from history that when they are backed into a corner, even when they are being killed, they are actually quite gracious. They embody to a T what it looks like to love one's enemies, to turn the other cheek.

Where did that come from?

Back then the Jewish people had a different idea of what revolution should look like. Almost two hundred years before Jesus is born, the Jews' number one hero is Judas Maccabee. He knows how to lead a proper revolution.

The story gets hot when a king named Antiochus Epiphanes is leading an attack on Israel, specifically the holy Temple. He and his pagan troops come into the Temple, into the Holy of Holies, and sacrifice a pig on the altar. He douses all the holy objects in the Temple with blood from this unclean animal. Epiphanes thinks he has desecrated that kosher Temple so thoroughly that no Jew will ever worship in it again.

What this Greek king does not anticipate, but will soon discover, is that the Israelites aren't going to take this lying down. A handful of them rise up and fight back against that giant army, and they win.

When any of those Jews do die—when the enemy army backs one of the Jewish revolutionaries into a corner, they die saying things much different than the Christians do two centuries later. They will die preaching about the resurrection, but with a different twist.

"You accursed wretch," one revolutionary hisses at the king who is killing him and his brothers. "You dismiss us from this present life, but the King of the universe will raise us up to an everlasting renewal of life, because we have died for his laws" (2 Macc. 7:9 RSV).

Right before the fourth brother draws his final breath, he defies his murderer: "One cannot but choose to die at the hands of men and to cherish the hope that God gives of being raised again by him. But for you there will be no resurrection to life!" (7:14 RSV).

The earliest Christians don't talk like this at all.

If all we knew about the early Christians was that when they died, they yelled down blessings instead of curses on those killing them, we'd know that something was drastically different about this group of people.

If all we knew about them was that they blessed those who hated them, we'd know that theirs is a very different kind of revolution.

Earlier, we looked at the life of Stephen, the first Christian martyr. When Stephen died, he didn't curse them. He died like the man he followed, by praying for the forgiveness of the very people who were killing him. But Acts tells us an interesting detail about this story: "And Saul was there, giving approval to his death" (8:1).

To me this is one of the most haunting verses in the Bible. Saul is standing there, watching this man being stoned. Saul steps on to the pages of human history, not as the famous church planter he will be remembered for, but as someone who is *fighting against Jesus*.

He doesn't have a huge part yet. He's just the coat boy, the valet for the murderers. But he sees it all. He witnesses Stephen's speech, he sees the religious leaders' rage, and he sees this good man die in a very different way.

I've wondered often what Saul is thinking when Stephen starts to call down blessings on the people killing him. That's got to be a bit disarming. Everyone there expects Stephen to return anger with anger, but he doesn't. I think it would soften up even the hardest critic to see and hear something like this, but apparently Saul just shakes it off.

Saul doesn't slow down a bit. He has seen someone respond to evil with raw goodness, and it doesn't seem to affect him at all. He just keeps pressing forward. He begins going from house to house trying to arrest as many Christians as he can catch.

License to Kill

What started with him holding coats while watching his partners stone a Christian has now progressed to Saul leading the assault on the Jesus followers. Luke tells us that Saul is planning on expanding his operation. He's going to Damascus to arrest and kill more Christians.

He has gone to the Jewish/Roman government puppet high priest and gotten a license to kill. He is like a Jewish James Bond.

Saul is nearing Damascus with power, with strength. But everything is about to change for him:

> As he neared Damascus on his journey, suddenly a light from heaven flashed around him. He fell to the ground and heard a voice say to him, "Saul, Saul, why do you persecute me?"
>
> "Who are you, Lord?" Saul asked.
>
> "I am Jesus, whom you are persecuting," he replied. "Now get up and go into the city, and you will be told what you must do."
>
> The men traveling with Saul stood there speechless; they heard the sound but did not see anyone. Saul got up from the ground, but when he opened his eyes he could see nothing. So they led him by the hand into Damascus. For three days he was blind, and did not eat or drink anything. (Acts 9:3–9)

Finally Saul meets Jesus, and he learns something interesting about him. Namely that Jesus isn't dead. Paul has been killing Christians because he thinks they are spreading lies about God. He really believes the stuff the other Pharisees circulate about Jesus, that he had died and the disciples had stolen his body. But Saul can't go on thinking that anymore.

Even more than that, Saul learns that this Jesus he has been opposing is still present.

Jesus asks Saul, "Why are you persecuting me?"

When Saul was helping to chunk rocks at a Christian's head, he didn't know he was aiming at Jesus.

Saul learns on the road that day that Jesus is the kind of God who identifies with the suffering and the oppressed. His conversation with Jesus is brief. Then God turns the lights out on Saul, and for three days Paul can't see a thing.

Now I hope the lights on your Bible dashboard are blinking right now.

Saul is blind for three days. Something else took three days, didn't it? This event is about something bigger than just God stopping murder. It's about the God of Jesus working to reconcile the whole world to himself. Which means reconciling people who had just recently been enemies.

In Damascus, there is a Christian leader named Ananias, someone who is probably on the hit list that Saul had been carrying with him. God appears to Ananias in a vision and tells him to go to the house of Judas and meet with Saul.

Now the name Judas has recently become unpopular in the circles that Ananias runs in, but it's the name Saul that stands out the most to Ananias. Ananias talks back to God; he gives him the latest news brief about what the word on the street is for Saul. He tells God, just in case he didn't know, that Saul is actually not one of the good guys.

Saul isn't wearing our jersey, and in fact, he is trying to arrest people like me.

Here's what God says: "But the Lord said to Ananias, 'Go! This man is my chosen instrument to carry my name before the Gentiles and their kings and before the people of Israel. I will show him how much he must suffer for my name'" (Acts 9:15–16).

And that's exactly what Ananias does. I know that there are a lot of miracles in the book of Acts that capture our imagination. People are healed in almost every chapter, demons are being kicked out, but I think one of the best miracles in Acts happens when Ananias first meets Saul face to face: he calls him brother.

His first words to a deadly enemy are those of radical welcome. They are words of family.

A Powerful Weakness

What is really interesting is what God tells Ananias about what he's going to use Saul for: to take his name to the kings of the earth and to Israel. One way Saul will do that is by suffering for Jesus' name.

God is going to use Saul, but in a way that often involves pain and danger instead of honor. Let that sink in for a moment, because in this one little sentence God is turning Saul's world upside down.

Until now in Saul's world, when God used you, sometimes that involved people suffering, but it wasn't you. The sufferers would have been the enemies of Israel. This is the way the world operates.

But it's not the way of Jesus.

The well-known pastor Eugene Peterson writes about how, as a child, he was bullied by another kid at school. His name was Garrison Johns, and he was relentless. Even as a child, Eugene Peterson had been immersed in the Christian life, so he knew the call of Jesus to turn the other cheek and love his enemies. But some enemies can be hard to love.

On one particular day, Eugene had had enough. When Garrison came after him, Peterson snapped. He fought back and quite successfully pinned the bully down, repeatedly pummeling him.

But now Eugene discovered that he didn't know how to end a fight.

So he reached back to his Christian upbringing and started yelling at Garrison Johns to "accept Jesus as his Lord and Savior." Eventually, Garrison wore down and started shouting out, "I accept Jesus as my Lord and Savior."

And this, Eugene Peterson says, "was my first Christian convert."[2]

We kind of intuitively know that this isn't the way to introduce someone to Jesus.

Jesus didn't come in power, at least not that kind of power. And what Saul is just starting to learn is how strong weakness can be. It's here that Paul starts to understand the implications of the cross. He learns that the cross isn't just the way God saved the world, but it's how he intends for his followers to carry out that salvation.

And this is something that Saul will spend the rest of his life trying to live out. Starting immediately. Look at what happens in the very next chapter:

> All those who heard him were astonished and asked,
> "Isn't he the man who raised havoc in Jerusalem among
> those who call on this name? And hasn't he come here to
> take them as prisoners to the chief priests?" Yet Saul grew
> more and more powerful and baffled the Jews living in
> Damascus by proving that Jesus is the Christ.
>
> After many days had gone by, the Jews conspired to
> kill him, but Saul learned of their plan. Day and night they
> kept close watch on the city gates in order to kill him.
> But his followers took him by night and lowered him in a
> basket through an opening in the wall. (Acts 9:21–25)

I love that Luke describes this moment by saying "Saul grew more and more powerful"; but I want us to pay attention to what this power looks like. He sneaks out of town. He gets lowered in a basket to get away from people who are trying to kill him.

If I was narrating this story, I would say that Saul was growing *less and less powerful.* Saul had entered Damascus with power. He came with all the authority of the Temple rulers to kill and arrest people. And then he has to escape from the town in a basket.

If this was a movie, it would be like it started off with Rambo and ended with Mary Poppins.

Later in Paul's ministry (long after his name-change) he finds himself writing to a church that is struggling with what it means to be the people of God. They want Paul to be more impressive, to show off a bit more. Paul writes to them to let them know how Jesus has turned his world upside down. In 2 Corinthians he tells them he has learned that when you are strong, then you are actually weak, but when you are weak, that's when you are really strong.

Do you want to know what story Paul uses to back up his point? This one. The story of his escaping death in a basket.

"If I must boast, I will boast of the things that show my weakness," Paul tells his converts. "The God and Father of the Lord Jesus, who is to be praised forever, knows that I am not lying. In Damascus the governor under King Aretas had the city of the Damascenes guarded in order to arrest me. But I was lowered in a basket from a window in the wall and slipped through his hands" (2 Cor. 11:30–33).

He brags about being weak.

Did you ever wonder why Saul changed his name to Paul? Does that seem odd to anyone else? I get changing your name, but take a lesson from pop culture. Try something like "Meta-World Peace." That's how you do it. You go all in. But Saul doesn't. He just changes one letter. Why?

I think it was because the name Saul was linked to the story of a king who tried to strong-arm his way through life. But *Paul* means something else entirely. It's Latin. It means *small*.

Saul laid down the heritage of the Jews' first king and became Paul, the small. And the rest of his life was spent living it out.

The War of the Lamb

When I was twelve years old, my parents and I went to visit my older brother and his new wife. When we walked into their home, the movie *Rambo: First Blood* was playing. Immediately, my mom said, "Curtis, we don't watch shows like that."

She was right. My parents never let shows like that on our family television. But the conversation moved on, and my brother didn't turn it off. And—I kid you not—not more than five minutes later, all of us are sitting around laughing and talking and we hear my mother yell at Rambo on the television screen: "Well, pick up the rock and kill him!"

This is how we have been taught to approach power. The bent of humanity has been to see this kind of matchup and think that might is right. But the Christian story is different.

Think about the way the Scriptures end.

In the book of Revelation we are introduced to the Dragon. Basically, Revelation says in this corner you've got this dragon with ten heads, and in the other corner you've got this little bitty lamb. And everyone would bet that the Dragon is going to win easily, but that's only because they don't know the power of the Lamb laying down his life.

In his book *Walking with God through Pain and Suffering*, Tim Keller tells of a time that John Dickson spoke in Australia once on the theme of the wounds of God. Here's how he tells it:

During the question time, a Muslim man rose to explain "how preposterous was the claim that the Creator of the universe should be subjected to the forces of his own creation—that he would have to eat, sleep, and go to the toilet, let alone die on a cross." Dickson said his remarks were intelligent, cogent, and civil. The man went on to argue that it was illogical that God, the "cause of all causes," could have pain inflicted on him by any lesser beings. The minister felt he had no knockdown argument, no witty comeback. So finally he simply thanked the man for making the uniqueness of the Christian claim so clear. "What the Muslim denounces as blasphemy the Christian holds precious: God has wounds."[3]

One of the greatest concerns I have about Christianity today is that we will pay attention to the victory of God through Jesus but ignore the way that Jesus is victorious.

Often, I hear us talking about Jesus the warrior, and that's right. In Revelation, Jesus is pictured as a warrior, riding on a white horse, covered in blood. But we must never forget that the blood on Jesus' knuckles is not someone else's. It is his own.

This is the kind of ministry God calls Paul to. It is the kind of ministry he calls all of us to.

The cross isn't just the way God saved the world, it's also how he calls us to partner with him. In a postmodern world, where truth is suspect and all big stories are seen as power plays, any claims to have a story big enough for everyone are always suspect. It's been said that history is written by the victors.

But we have a story that holds up as the greatest victory—a defeated Jewish carpenter. And we say that's power.

C. S. Lewis said that one of the greatest temptations of the church is to trade grace for power. I think it's because we have forgotten that grace is power. But it is a very different kind of power. One that doesn't operate from a top-down mentality, but finds its greatest strength in serving.

This changes the way we enter into conversations. It changes the way we look at our relationships. It changes the way we live, and it changes the way we die.

Welcome to the Kingdom of God, where God's people trade titles for baskets. Where God himself chooses mangers over thrones.

Where weak is the new strong.

Chapter 9

You're Going to Need a Bigger Box

"Left to ourselves, we tend immediately to reduce God to manageable terms. We want to get Him where we can use Him, or at least know where He is when we need Him. We want a God we can in some measure control."
    —A. W. Tozer

"This God we have made and because we have made him we can understand him; because we have created him he can never surprise us, never overwhelm us, nor astonish us, nor transcend us."
    —A. W. Tozer

Igrew up in a church of ten people. Most people would call that a small group, but it was my entire church. We had a building and services and everything, and I love the people from that church.

When I went to college, I would come back a few times a year to preach, and I would try to bring some friends with me to encourage my church family. One of those Sundays we had brought about forty people with us, and right before it was time for me to preach, Brother Foy, the patriarch of the church, stood up to introduce me.

Which is funny in itself, because I was the only person there who knew everyone. This was the church I grew up in, and these were my friends who came home with me. But tradition is tradition, and if someone other than Foy was preaching, he was going to say something.

So Foy stood up and the first words out of his mouth were, "I can't help but notice that all of our guests are white." And I was wondering where this was going. Because Foy was crazy. He was crazy for Jesus, but he was crazy. If he felt like something was true, he would say it without regard for how you felt about it, and I could tell this was about to be one of those occasions.

"We have forty extra people with us this morning, and not one of them is a colored person." Then Foy pointed at the African-American teenage boy sitting on the second row and said, "I brought a Negro this morning. Why didn't you?" (Obviously, political correctness was not Foy's strong suit.)

"Now Brother Jonathan, come preach the word to us."

I've heard of some crummy introductions in the past, but try topping that one.

I had to stand up and preach to a group of people who were just made to feel as if they were the von Trapp family. Now, to be fair, we had invited several people from different races and backgrounds to come with us, and for one reason or another they couldn't come that day.

One of my African-American friends had slept in, and later we were pretty hard on him. Thanks for making us look like bigots today.

But to be honest, looking back, I'm glad Brother Foy asked that question. I wish all our churches had someone asking, "Do we all look the same?"

And here's why.

We've seen in our study so far that church (actually religion in general) tends to tilt and turn in on itself—to be absorbed in what happens within its own walls or tribe.

This is part of what makes the book of Acts so inspiring. You've got these people whose faith is so big, so magnificent, that there's not a box big enough to hold it in.

But not all of Acts is like that.

Chariots and Fire

One of the minor characters in Acts is a guy named Philip. He plays a small role, but don't let that fool you, because God does some huge things with Philip's life.

On the day when he ascends to heaven, Jesus commissions his disciples to be witnesses of his resurrection all over the world. This would have seemed like an impossible task. In a time when most people did not travel further than thirty miles from their birthplace, Jesus was sending people all over the world.

But when people start dying for their faith in Jesus, the early converts begin retreating from the center of the conflict. Lots of Christians hit the road, going back to their homes in the seventeen provinces listed in Acts 1, and beyond.

That's when we first read about Philip in the book of Acts. He's gone north to Samaria, a place he (like most Jews in that era) probably grew up hating. He's getting a quick and mind-blowing education. Now he's learning that God loves Samaritans too. And, as if God hasn't stretched Philip enough, God does this:

> Now an angel of the Lord said to Philip, "Go south to the
> road—the desert road—that goes down from Jerusalem
> to Gaza." So he started out, and on his way he met an
> Ethiopian eunuch, an important official in charge of all the

treasury of Candace, queen of the Ethiopians. This man had gone to Jerusalem to worship, and on his way home was sitting in his chariot reading the book of Isaiah the prophet. (Acts 8:26–28)

A couple of things you need to know about this eunuch fellow. Back then it was common practice that, if a man was going to be a high-ranking officer under a woman such as a queen, he had to become a eunuch. And you thought you sacrificed a lot for your job!

Maybe it was voluntary, maybe it wasn't. But it has paid off. Now he's driving a chariot, which was the equivalent of a private jet in the ancient world. He's rich enough to know how to read in a world that was mostly illiterate, and he even owns a portion of the scroll of Isaiah.

But now he's searching for more. He's traveling to a foreign Temple to worship a foreign God. And it's on his way home that he finds out that he isn't just searching for God. God is searching for him.

God sends Philip to the eunuch's chariot for the world's first high-speed Bible study, and Philip discovers that the eunuch is reading the book of Isaiah.

Which is significant, because Luke has been repeatedly making allusions to or quoting from Isaiah. In fact, Luke quotes from Isaiah more than any other book in the New Testament. And he really focuses on the good parts, the highlights. Acts is like the SportsCenter of Isaiah.

But what is really significant is the passage the eunuch is reading. It's about the Suffering Servant, the person he's going to find out is named Jesus. But it's also a passage about hope, about God setting things right. And look what is in this same section of Isaiah.

Let no foreigner who has bound himself to the LORD say,
> "The LORD will surely exclude me from his people."
And let not any eunuch complain,

"I am only a dry tree."
For this is what the LORD says:
"To the eunuchs who keep my Sabbaths,
　　who choose what pleases me
　　and hold fast to my covenant—
to them I will give within my temple and its walls
　　a memorial and a name
　　better than sons and daughters;
I will give them an everlasting name that will not be
　　cut off." (Isa. 56:3–5)

Back in that time, your legacy, your hope, is in your offspring. So if you can't have children, you are worthless. You're hopeless. And God is saying to eunuchs like this one that this is not true. He says, "I'll give you a name that will be remembered."

You know this eunuch has traveled to Jerusalem to go to the Temple and worship. But when he got there, he probably found out about the verse in Deuteronomy 23:1, "No one who has been emasculated by crushing or cutting may enter the assembly of the LORD."

This guy travels hundreds of miles to meet with God, and when he gets there, he finds out that he can't even go inside God's house. And maybe that's why the eunuch asks Philip if he can be baptized.

If you listen closely to this question, it's got an ache to it. It's a question that is anticipating rejection. "Why shouldn't I be baptized?"

Now Philip actually grew up with a really good answer to that question. This guy can't become a convert because he's a eunuch. That's why he couldn't go into the Temple. Here's this conservative Jewish guy who has spent most of his life learning the Torah, learning the Jewish rules, and now he's talking with an African eunuch who wants to become a part of the people of God.

When the eunuch asks what keeps him from being baptized, the correct answer is, "A lot of things, actually." Philip knows that if he baptizes this guy, he's breaking some ancient taboos, but he also knows that God has led him to this man for a reason.

What do you do when you realize that God is bigger than the religion you've grown up trying to serve him in? What do you do when God tells you to do what he has told you not to do?

This is the central struggle for the early church. They wrestle with decision after decision about what it means to be the people of God in an era when so many of the rules seem to have changed.[1]

Repeatedly, they're wondering what to do, not because their old faith was bad, but because God is doing something fresh and new in Jesus. And this isn't just Philip's dilemma. This happens with almost every Christian leader.

Like a few chapters later in Acts 10.

Pigs in a Blanket

Peter is chilling out on a friend's flat-roof patio, and he has a dream. It's a strange vision from God about all sorts of animals that were blacklisted as unclean to the Jewish people. In the vision, a menagerie of forbidden critters come down in a sheet. Side note: Is this where we got the idea for Pigs in a Blanket? Just wondering.

You probably know this story. God tells Peter to butcher one of these animals and eat it. After all, it's lunch time.

And Peter says no to God, which is always a bad idea. But the reason he gives is interesting. He says, "I've never eaten what was unclean." In other words, "I've always kept the rules *you* gave us." Which is something I can relate to.

When I was in high school, my best friend "Bub" and I made a pact never again to watch an R-rated movie. It was a convenient pact for us to make, because growing up in a conservative home, we weren't allowed to watch such movies, and now we got the added bonus of feeling spiritual about avoiding them. But then when I was in college, *The Passion of the Christ* came to the theaters. And, just to stick it to me, Mel Gibson had it rated R. So now I've got Jesus himself starring in an R-rated movie. Now what do we do?

I bet this is how Peter felt.

God's response is great.

"The voice spoke to him a second time, 'Do not call anything impure that God has made clean'" (Acts 10:15). God basically responds by saying, "Look, Buster, that's my call." How do you come back to that? God is telling Peter to do something that God earlier had told him not to do. Peter has always thought such a diet was wrong, and now he finds out he can have ham sandwiches.

For Peter, grace tastes a lot like bacon.

Of course, the point of Peter's dream is not really about food. God wants to get Peter thinking about who decides what is unclean or clean. Notice that Peter doesn't eat. Instead he gets picked up by a few visitors who have been sent to take him up the coast to see a fellow named Cornelius.

Luke tells us Cornelius is a Roman centurion and a God-fearer.

Which means he's not a Jew. He doesn't watch *Shalom* in his home. He doesn't even watch *Seinfeld*.

Cornelius received a vision earlier in the chapter. In it, God told him where to go find Peter. So these two very different men have two different visions. God is trying to draw them together. And when they do get together, Cornelius reveals just how different their worlds are. Cornelius bows down to Peter, and Peter awkwardly corrects him. "I am just a man . . . and in this story we don't worship people."

While he is giving "How to stop being a pagan" lessons, a crowd starts to gather, and Peter has to give one of the most uncomfortable speeches in the Bible. Peter says, "You all know, it's against our law for a Jew to even associate or visit with a Gentile." Which probably isn't the best way to introduce oneself. But it was true. There were all kinds of rumors going around back then about each group. Gentiles said that Jews were lazy (because of the Sabbath) and atheists (because they didn't worship all the gods). And Jews wouldn't go into Gentile homes because they said that they performed abortions in there.

But Peter in one swift move has broken the biggest taboo in Israel's code.

But what else could he do? God had sent a vision to the Roman centurion telling him how to get to Peter, and a vision to Peter to tell him how to treat Cornelius when he got there. And that's when the very thing that we think he should have known all along finally begins to dawn on Peter:

> Then Peter began to speak: "I now realize how true it is that God does not show favoritism but accepts men from every nation who fear him and do what is right. You know the message God sent to the people of Israel, telling the good news of peace through Jesus Christ, who is Lord of all." (Acts 10:34–36)

Peter says God is no respecter of persons. That is huge for Peter to say. We hear that and think, "Yeah, that sounds about right." But until this point everyone thought that's exactly what God was—a respecter of persons. He liked some people more than others.

But here in this moment it finally clicks for Peter and, with the help of the vision the Lord sent the day before, he has this profound realization that God is no respecter of persons because Jesus is Lord of all.

Saving the Saved

Now I want you to think about Peter here. When he first met Jesus, one of the things he wanted more than any other was to destroy Rome. When Jesus is arrested in the garden, Peter pulls his sword on the army this guy represents.

Now here in this moment Peter isn't just befriending a Gentile. He's rubbing shoulders with the very enemy he'd once hated.

Did you ever wonder when Peter really gets it?

Because if you think about it, Peter has more conversion experiences than probably any other person in Scripture. When he first meets Jesus, when he tries to correct Jesus, when he denies Jesus, and now in Acts 10, Peter's world is being turned upside down all over again.

Here is one of the main themes for those earliest Christians. God is changing the whole world, but he is also changing his people.

In Acts, so many people are coming to know the Lord. God keeps drawing all these people back to himself. But in almost every episode, you see God not just converting the pagans, but also his own people.

For example, I think it's interesting to notice that baptism wasn't new to Christians. Jews had been using it for hundreds of years. It was a symbol of passing through the waters of the Exodus, and when a Gentile wanted to become a Jew, they would make them get baptized.

But the book of Acts starts off with over three thousand people being baptized. And here's the kicker: they were all Jews! They were already "in," they were "saved," they belonged to the family of God. And Peter tells them all to convert. After all, at this point Peter has started to learn that conversion is not just something that happened; it is something that keeps happening.

God starts off this story of the early church, not by converting the pagans, but by converting his own people.

For the past few generations many of us have had a pretty stagnant view of conversion. We've viewed it as a one-time event; and on some level it is, but Scripture has a more layered view of it, as if it's more of a process.

Now I know that some of us may have grown up fearing that we weren't saved, and that's a shame. All of us need to hear that we are secure with God.

God is not fickle, and he doesn't sit around just waiting on us to mess up. But some of us have reduced the gospel of Jesus to nothing more than salvation from hell. The reason we are tempted to do this may have been identified by Tolstoy. He said, "Everyone wants to change the world, no one wants to change themselves."

Which makes me think back to Brother Foy telling us we should have brought people different than ourselves. Around thirty years earlier, when Foy had already been a Christian for a decade or two, he became convicted that he was a racist. And for Foy that was unacceptable. So he moved to an all-black town and spent the rest of his career teaching at an all-black school.

He lived out the word repentance to a T.

He often took me and a few other younger guys to black churches, just so we could rub shoulders with people we weren't familiar with, just to see how much we had in common. From the time when I met Foy, he had African-Americans living in his house with him, and he had a black brother with him that morning at church.

Now we could argue that he had tried that morning to superimpose his journey on our own. But I want you to know the conviction that good man lived out in front of me was one of the primary forces that shaped me while I was growing up.

Foy challenged all of us in that church to grow up in Christ to a new level of commitment and understanding.

Jesus wants to save Christians too.

He wants to save us from being racist, or materialistic.

He wants to save us from thinking this whole thing is about us.

He wants to save us from losing sight of how big the whole story really is.

Conversion isn't just for people who don't know God; it's also for those of us who do.[2]

Which is why Peter's sermon at Cornelius' home ends the way it does. They all hear these Gentile Christians speaking in tongues and praising God and Peter asks, "Can anyone keep these people from being baptized with water?"

It is a question Peter would have answered differently just a few days ago, but now God has changed Peter.

Just a few days before this, Peter would have given you a list of reasons why this was wrong. Now Peter knows that God is up to something much bigger than just Peter's own race. Now Peter isn't asking why shouldn't they be baptized. He's asking, can anyone stop this even if they tried?

God Never Had a Box

In the religious tribe that I belong to, we have tended to read the book of Acts as if it could be broken down into a series of steps or a law code of some kind, all the while forgetting the most basic message Acts is telling.

We seemed to miss Luke's grand truth that God is untamed, undomesticated, and refuses to fit neatly into any worldview or system.

Several decades ago a guy named Thomas Kuhn invented the word *paradigm*. He said a paradigm is a way of looking at or understanding the world. Different people call it different things, such as a worldview or a mindset.

The analogy Kuhn used to describe it is interesting, I think. He said that our worldviews, our paradigms, are like constellations of stars. We look up and see a billion stars in the sky and are overwhelmed. So we invent constellations as ways of wrapping our minds around something that is far bigger than we are.

Constellations are really like a box in which we pack limited groups of stars so we can examine and understand them. But God help us if we ever look up into the sky with its billions and billions of stars and see only Orion's Belt. God help us if we get so stunted in our perspective that we can see only one box.

And God help us if we ever forget that, for all our fancy boxes, God is bigger than any single worldview or mindset.

No box is big enough to contain him.

Luke talks about the Temple a lot, and most of the time he's pretty hard on it. Not because it was bad, but because it was incomplete. People started thinking that since the Temple was where God was, it was where God must stay.

So what started out as a way to meet God became a way to domesticate God. Do you remember Stephen's (the first martyr) last words?

The Most High does not live in houses made by men. As the prophet says:

"'Heaven is my throne,
    and the earth is my footstool.
What kind of house will you build for me?'
        says the Lord.
    'Or where will my resting place be?
Has not my hand made all these things?'" (Acts 7:48–50)

If your religion ever becomes an effort to fit God into a box, then you're going to need a bigger box. No box, no matter how big or golden or shiny it is, can contain God. And the truth is, as much as we might like to think otherwise, God has never fit in a box.

When I was a sophomore in college, I remember sitting in a missions class at Harding University listening to a story that would change my life.

My professor, Dr. Monte Cox, and his family had been missionaries in Kenya for over a decade. When they moved there, it had not been popular with their family. Monte and his wife Beth had just had their first child, and their parents were heartbroken to be separated so soon from their only grandchild.

For years Monte's family did not visit them in Africa. Then finally they made the long trip to Kenya. On their first Sunday there, Monte was introducing his dad to all the people at one of the village churches they had planted. Somehow it got out that his parents didn't initially want them to leave the States.

One of the African women who heard this ran up to Monte and asked him to translate a story for his father. She told Monte's dad how, when she was a little girl, her grandfather had sat down their whole family and told them that one day a white man would come to this area of the world, and that this white man would tell them a story about God. And, while he didn't know if he would be alive when this person came to their village, her grandfather told them he had had this vision and wanted them to believe the story the white man told them, because God was sending him to them.

This was the first time Monte had heard this story. As he was translating what the village woman was saying to his dad, it began to dawn on them both that, as painful as the separation had been, this whole story was far bigger than they had previously realized.

I still remember what chair I was sitting in when I heard that story. Up until that moment in my life, I had reduced God to a good idea or a history lesson. Suddenly, I began to see that if that's who God is, then I'm going to need a bigger box.

I don't have categories for stories like this. There are not any systematic theologies that stories like this fit into very neatly.

But this is the story of Acts.

Luke is telling us how God is drawing all these people to himself—pagans and Christians converting. He is telling us how God is piecing the world back together, one person at a time.

And behind it all is the resurrection. When they buried Jesus, they shut his body up in that tomb and sealed it with the best stone a rich man could afford. But the resurrection is God's ultimate way of telling us, if you are going to contain me, you're going to need a bigger box.

Chapter 10

Between the Doors

"Prayer does not stop with the 'Amen.' It rises to its feet and walks off, with our built up yearning turned into action. . . . The Lord's Prayer is not intercession. It is enlistment."

—Scot McKnight

When I was a junior in college, I went with some friends to West Memphis to see an opera.

There was a girl involved. Obviously. Unfortunately, we were not able to find the opera house, and it was getting late. And we were getting hungry. So we found ourselves driving around looking for some place to eat.

Finally, we found a mall that had a food court and a merry-go-round. The merry-go-round was closed. But no mall security rope was going to stop us. We climbed over the rope and wandered around the merry-go-round. A really rough couple of lawbreakers.

Almost immediately some mall police officers ran out, yelling for us to get off the merry-go-round. So we did. My friend and I started walking away, and the cops started chasing us, shouting that we were under arrest. Which is not something I wanted on my résumé.

The security guys hauled us into a back room and started barking about how we were going to jail for trespassing. And I sat there blank-eyed, thinking about what that experience might look like. You know, sitting in a cell talking with the other criminals about what we're in the slammer for. I pictured a guy telling me he was in there for drug abuse, maybe another guy talking about being locked up for robbing a 7/11, and then me, telling them I was in there for being on a merry-go-round.

I'm not proud of this, but I played the preacher card. I hoped it would be a Get-Out-of-Jail-Free card. I told them that I sure hoped I got out of jail in time to preach the next morning (which was true).

"Wait, you're a preacher?" They were surprised. I saw my opportunity, so I took it. I asked them, "Are you Christians?"

And, to be honest, this was in Arkansas in the 1990s, so there wasn't a lot of chance that they were going to say, "Nope, we're Buddhists." When they said "Yes," I immediately said, "Let's pray."

To which they responded shyly, "Yes . . . that's what we always do. . . . We always pray with the people we arrest."

I've always had a bit of an awkward relationship to prayer. I wrestle with how to do it, how it works, or (if I'm being honest) even if it works. I like to do stuff, and sometimes it seems like people use prayer to avoid life (or manipulate security guards). But in the Scriptures, it seems that prayer isn't divorced from action, often prayer is what leads to it.

Prayer Partners

When we open up Genesis 2, God has just created the entire universe, and he's done a good job. But now Genesis throws in a detail that I think most of us have read over so often that we've stopped seeing its significance.

God makes Adam, and even in this grand creation that God consistently describes as "good," he notices something that isn't good.

God says that "it is not good for man to be alone."

So God starts a parade of animals past Adam to see if any of them will help Adam not be lonely. It is the world's first speed-dating session. It's a weird mixture of "Animal Planet" and "The Bachelor."

Almost as a side note, God has Adam name the animals. That's a big job.

When our son was born, my wife and I had the hardest time coming up with a name for him. We didn't want to mess this up. My friend Josh Graves pointed out that while names do matter, unless we named him Adolf Herod, we should be fine. Although, if we name him Bubba, he's never going to be curator at the Louvre.

Naming is a big responsibility.

Up until now, the Lord has been naming everything. He did a good job with the naming the light thing. He did fine when he decided to call the light part "day" and the dark part "night."

Why does God now want Adam to take over? Surely God's creative juices are not tapped out.

Instead, I think this is what God has had in mind all along: a partnership with Adam and with all the humans who will come after him.

According to the Jewish scholar Abraham Heschel, one of the main themes of the Scriptures is the *Mitzvot*. We translate that Hebrew word as *good works*, but it conveys more than that. It imparts the idea of partnering with God.

Now this isn't a fifty/fifty partnership to be sure. It's not that God even needs a partner. But it's all through Scripture.

Getting Our Feet Wet

For example, early in the book of Joshua when God invites the people of Israel to cross over the Jordan River, God promises them that he's going to part that roaring, flood-stage river for them. God is going to do it, but to make it happen the priests' feet must touch the water.

God doesn't do this because those holy men have magic feet. He does this because he's looking for people to trust him and to join in what he is doing.

Let me point out right here that this concept is especially true in prayer. Have you ever heard stories about God answering huge prayers for people, and you thought to yourself, yeah right (cue eye roll). You know, you hear somebody telling about some kid whose arm grew back in Uganda, and you just happened not to be there to see it. If that kind of stuff happens, you have to wonder, why am I never there? And furthermore, why does God never seem to answer my prayer for something like making my flu go away?

I think part of the answer to questions like these is another question: What are we doing with our lives that requires God to participate? Or maybe a better question is: Have you ever been doing something beyond yourself and found yourself thinking that there is no way this is going to work out unless God does something?

And then he does it?

Dallas Willard talks about this kind of belief this way: "The cautious faith that never saws off the limb on which it is sitting never learns that unattached limbs may find strange, unaccountable ways of not falling."[1]

It is all too possible to do a lot of religious activities that don't depend on God at all. And those things can actually tick God off.

Think about the times that the prophets critique God's people because their religions assemblies and ceremonies are not connected to what they are doing in the other parts of their lives. Like in Isaiah where God and Israel have a conversation:

> "Why have we fasted," they say,
>> "and you have not seen it?
> Why have we humbled ourselves,
>> and you have not noticed?"
> Yet on the day of your fasting, you do as you please
>> and exploit all your workers.
> Your fasting ends in quarreling and strife,
>> and in striking each other with wicked fists.
> You cannot fast as you do today
>> and expect your voice to be heard on high. (Isa. 58:3–4)

Prayer is important, Isaiah recognizes, but prayer was never meant to operate on its own. Prayer is always a part of something bigger. I don't know of a better, or funnier, story to illustrate this than Acts 12.

Prison Break

> It was about this time that King Herod arrested some who belonged to the church, intending to persecute them. He had James, the brother of John, put to death with the sword. When he saw that this pleased the Jews, he proceeded to seize Peter also. This happened during the Feast of Unleavened Bread. After arresting him, he put him in prison, handing him over to be guarded by four squads of four soldiers each. Herod intended to bring him out for public trial after the Passover.
>
> So Peter was kept in prison, but the church was earnestly praying to God for him. (Acts 12:1–5)

Acts 12 opens with Herod Agrippa I. He is a client king, which means he is not true royalty. He answers to Caesar, and his job, like the other Herods before him, is to keep Israel happy but subdued. And, to be honest, he's doing okay. Of all the Herods, Agrippa shows the most respect for the Jews' customs.

When he has James, one of Jesus' original disciples, arrested and killed, the king sees that this pleases the local religious leaders. So when he realizes that this might raise his numbers in the polls, he decides to take out Peter, too.

This is a purely political move. Making the people happy makes his job secure. So everyone wins. Everyone except Peter.

Peter is about to be killed by the same immoral system Jesus was killed by a few years before him. During Passover, Herod's henchmen are working to throw together some pretense of a trial. Herod knows the Christians have a reputation for prison breaks. So he's taking special measures to keep Peter from pulling some kind of Houdini trick.

Peter is under maximum security. Four squads of soldiers are guarding him, and he's chained to two soldiers at once.

All the time.

This is the ancient world equivalent of being on death row at Alcatraz. It looks like Peter is about to be executed just as James was. He has no hope. The church's top apostle is chained in a dungeon waiting to die.

But Luke tells us the church is praying for him.

> The night before Herod was to bring him to trial, Peter
> was sleeping between two soldiers, bound with two
> chains, and sentries stood guard at the entrance. Suddenly
> an angel of the Lord appeared and a light shone in the cell.
> He struck Peter on the side and woke him up. "Quick, get
> up!" he said, and the chains fell off Peter's wrists.

Then the angel said to him, "Put on your clothes and sandals." And Peter did so. "Wrap your cloak around you and follow me," the angel told him. Peter followed him out of the prison, but he had no idea that what the angel was doing was really happening; he thought he was seeing a vision. They passed the first and second guards and came to the iron gate leading to the city. It opened for them by itself, and they went through it. When they had walked the length of one street, suddenly the angel left him.

Then Peter came to himself and said, "Now I know without a doubt that the Lord sent his angel and rescued me from Herod's clutches and from everything the Jewish people were anticipating." (Acts 12:6–11)

The angel struck him? So "touched by an angel" isn't always a good thing. This angel starts giving Peter commands as he leads him out of this maximum security prison. This sounds like an episode of "24" mixed with "30 Rock."

My favorite line so far in this episode is that Peter has no idea that this is really happening. Peter looks kind of like a moron here, but we've all had moments like this, times when we wake up but we're not sure what's going on.

When I was a freshman in college, I woke up in the middle of the night with three guys standing over me with a razor and shaving cream. They had decided to pull a prank on me by shaving my eyebrows. Needless to say, I was surprised.

But no one could tell that I was.

Something like that is going on here. Peter is just waking up in the middle of an angelic prison break, so let's give Peter the benefit of the doubt for not catching on immediately. Let's also pay attention to the bizarre nature of this story. Peter is delivered from prison. The angel gets him out of a really tight spot. Then suddenly the angel vanishes. He leaves Peter on the side of the street in the middle of the night.

That's when Peter, who until now has been a bit slow on the uptake, realizes that he's no longer a prisoner. But he is a fugitive.

> When this had dawned on him, he went to the house of Mary the mother of John, also called Mark, where many people had gathered and were praying. Peter knocked at the outer entrance, and a servant girl named Rhoda came to answer the door. When she recognized Peter's voice, she was so overjoyed she ran back without opening it and exclaimed, "Peter is at the door!"
>
> "You're out of your mind," they told her. When she kept insisting that it was so, they said, "It must be his angel."
>
> But Peter kept on knocking, and when they opened the door and saw him, they were astonished. Peter motioned with his hand for them to be quiet and described how the Lord had brought him out of prison. "Tell James and the brothers about this," he said, and then he left for another place.
>
> In the morning, there was no small commotion among the soldiers as to what had become of Peter. After Herod had a thorough search made for him and did not find him, he cross-examined the guards and ordered that they be executed.
>
> Then Herod went from Judea to Caesarea and stayed there a while. (Acts 12:12–19)

This story is brilliant! Because we know exactly what this is like. This is one of the things I appreciate about Acts. It doesn't present the early Christians as infallible, perfect people. They are people who are capable of great acts of faith in one moment and then great acts of stupidity in the next.

In other words, they are people like us.

How many of us have had moments like this one in Acts 12? How often have we sat in prayer meetings asking God for something we don't think there is a chance he's going to do. And remember, this is happening during Passover time.

Passover celebrates a time in Israel's history when God frees his people. It was when he freed Shadrach, Meshach, and Abednego from the fiery furnace. It was when he freed Daniel from the den of lions.

These Jewish Christians in Acts 12 know those stories inside and out, but they don't think those long-past tales have anything to do with what is going on right now in their time of crisis.

I think their problem is our problem.

Those Christians gathered in Mary's home have bought into the idea that they are praying to a God who used to act. They believe that God did great things in the past, that God used to be really active.

But that concept of God is foreign to the Bible. All through Scripture, God still acts. He still wants his people to partner with him.

But these believers in Mary's house evidently don't believe. They are on their knees, urgently praying for Peter, when Rhoda comes in and announces, "Hey, he's here!" To which they reply, "Shut up. Can't you see that we are praying for Peter to get out of jail?" But they obviously don't expect him to be freed.

Where is Peter while all of this is going on?

At the front door.

He's got the keys to the Kingdom, but not the keys to Mary's house.

The Lord's Prayer

One time Jesus' disciples ask him to teach them to pray. So he does. He teaches them probably the best-known prayer today. But do you know that Jesus doesn't just reinvent the wheel here?

He actually uses a famous Jewish prayer known as the Kaddish. He does make some significant revisions, however, and one of the biggest is this. Jesus removes the Amen.

Now that may sound like it's not a big deal, but I want you to imagine what it would do to our concept of being the people of God if we followed this. The danger of saying Amen is that, if we let it, this word can subconsciously insinuate that our part in the whole prayer process is over.

The Lord's Prayer is a revolutionary prayer. We are, after all, asking that God's Kingdom come to earth.

We are asking that things would be on earth as they are in heaven, where there is no death, oppression, tsunamis, or Oklahoma Sooner fans. When we pray this famous prayer, we are asking a whole lot. And it, in turn, asks a whole lot of us.

I like Scot McKnight's observation about this: "Prayer does not stop with the 'Amen.' It rises to its feet and walks off, with our built-up yearning turned into action." He counsels us: "The Lord's Prayer is not intercession. It is enlistment."[2]

But when was the last time you said the Lord's Prayer without the Amen? We've added it back in, haven't we? And here's why I think we did that.

It's because we have learned how to compartmentalize our lives into neat little divided sections. For an hour a week we are followers of Jesus, we believe the most revolutionary things, we love our enemies, we turn the other cheek.

For that hour we live in an upside-down Kingdom. Then we say Amen.

But what if Jesus removed this word intentionally? What if Jesus' idea was for us to talk to God, to get his vision for what the world could be like, and then to go out and put skin on it?

I think in the Sermon on the Mount Jesus is teaching us that this is what Kingdom-praying people live like.

Responding to Our Prayers

I was well into high school when I had my first girlfriend. Her name was Ashley, and she met all my qualifications for dating. (By "qualifications," I mean that she liked me somewhat.)

Almost immediately, I was infatuated with Ashley; and almost as immediately, Ashley's family moved to Colorado. This was back when long-distance phone calls actually cost money. After the first phone bill came in, my parents flipped out because I had run up over one hundred dollars in charges (and because Mom and Dad just didn't get love).

Since I was now forbidden to call the love of my life, I was forced to do what every other boy who was a teenager in the 1990s did. I made Ashley a mix-tape.

I played the sappiest, cheesiest love songs that I knew. In my better moments, I let the artists sing. In my more stupid moments, I sang along with them. I would end each tape I sent by telling Ashley how much I loved her, and then I would let Boys 2 Men take it home.

Every night I would get on my knees and pray for Ashley. Today, I still pray for her, but now I pray that she has lost those mix-tapes and that Ashley never puts anything on Facebook. But back then I would pray every night and say, "God, if you're really there, then please, please let me marry Ashley. And, while we're at it, I'd like to become an astronaut."

I'm thankful that the Spirit intercedes for us when we pray. I imagine that the Spirit was hearing my prayers and communicating to God that this dumb kid doesn't have a clue what he wants. One day he's going to meet the love of his life. And don't make him an astronaut. He's scared of heights.

But this is how we often approach prayer, as a grocery list of needs. And I am thankful indeed that the Spirit intercedes for us.

But I think the Spirit intercedes for God, too.

I've been to India and Sri Lanka and Nepal and several Third World countries. When I ask these people who have little or no resources what Christians in our prosperous land can do for them, their first response always is to ask us to pray for them. I almost always am tempted to say, "Yes, but you know we really want to help. What can we *really* do for you?"

But for them prayer isn't abandoning responsibility. Prayer is opening up ourselves to the Kingdom and to the will of God.

Eugene Peterson cautions us: "Be slow to pray." Then he explains, "Praying puts us at risk of getting involved with God's conditions. Praying most often doesn't get us what we want but what God wants. Something quite at variance with what we conceive to be in our best interests. And when we realize what is going on, it is often too late to go back."[3]

If the early Christians had stopped praying for the widows and orphans, they might have stopped caring for them. What prayer does is to open us up to God's desire for the world. And then it gets us to be a part of it. Prayer and activism have to go hand in hand. If they don't, we will have inactive believers and worn-out activists.

God isn't looking just for people to pray. He's looking for people to partner with him. In other words, God delivers Peter—he answers their prayers—but somebody's got to get the door.

This is part of what it means to be the church.

We pray for God to bring heaven to earth, and then we open our eyes to partner with him in doing just that.

You know the one problem with the book of Acts? It's filled with unfinished stories. We never find out what happens to Peter that day. The story leaves us with all kinds of questions.

This happens often.

Luke closes the book by telling us Paul is on trial for his life. Then the screen fades to black. It's like watching a play and right at the climatic moment the curtain falls.

You're left wondering what happened. Does the top keep spinning? Is it a dream or reality? Is the island real or not?

Do you want to know why Acts does that? It's because this story isn't over.

We're asking God what happens next, and God is saying, "You are."

Prayer doesn't just change God; it changes us, too.

Do you remember that time when Jesus is teaching thousands of people, and they get hungry? Then he tells the disciples to feed them. And they know they can't go hit up the local Wal-Mart and get food for all these people. So they tell the Lord they don't have enough. "What do you have?" Jesus asks them. Then he proceeds to take their sack of fish and chips and feeds the crowd.

Plenty of people want to change the world with their own power. Plenty of people are waiting on God to change the world. But the story Scripture tells us is about a God who works through us.

We live between the doors. God opens the door to Peter's cell. He waits for his people to quit praying long enough to open Mary's door. You and I live between those doors.

We live with a God who is waiting on us to be pray-ers and then partners. In the name of Jesus.

Chapter 11

How to Stop a Riot

"When God sets out to embrace the enemy, the result is the cross . . . Having been embraced by God, we must make space for others . . . even our enemies."

—Miroslav Volf[1]

"This is God's table. Who are we to check the guest list?"

—Madeleine L'Engle's favorite invitation to Communion[2]

A pastor named Rob Bell wrote a book. And he made a video about this book. Kind of a teaser covering what the book would be about. In this video he asks some questions.

But apparently they are not questions a lot of people think we should be asking. So in just one Saturday afternoon, Rob Bell, this widely known Christian pastor, becomes the number one trending Twitter topic. He cruises right past Justin Bieber and Lady Gaga.

This popular preacher gets crucified by a group of Christian leaders who disagree with his theology. So, in the course of one lazy weekend, Rob Bell basically becomes a millionaire from book pre-sales. And the critics' blog traffic goes through the roof.

Everyone appears to be a winner. But the Jesus story takes a hit.

This negative impact is seen especially by another guy on Twitter, a fellow also named Rob Bell, who unfortunately had been using the Twitter handle @RobBell.

This second Rob Bell keeps wondering, "Why is everyone so angry with me?"

It's funny, until you consider that a thousand stories like this happen every day. It seems as if we live in a time where people get angry about nearly any idea expressed about any subject.

Acts of Reconciliation

People who open Acts for the first time often are surprised to see how often the earliest Christians found themselves in the center of riots. The gospel put those first believers at odds with the politics, the economics, and many of the values of their day.

They were deeply at odds with the status quo, so they often mixed things up.

By outsiders they were seen as people who were enemies of the way things were. They were perceived as agents of change. But by their fellow-believers they were welcomed as humble and hospitable people. They were people who made great concessions in order to live peaceably in community.

One of the great ironies of today's world is that this perception of Christians has been reversed.

Churches today tend to be known by many as bastions of conservatism. We followers of Jesus are seen by modern media as people who easily sanction the way things are. But on the inside—within our own ranks—we often are seen as people who are volatile and sensitive, prone to easy eruptions.

As I study the book of Acts, I find myself wondering if one of the first things we as churches have to learn in order to start a riot is how to stop one.

Let me explain.

Once this Jesus movement started to pick up some steam, the earliest Christians began running into all sorts of problems. They were converting people from every kind of religious and pagan background and were finding themselves wrestling with all kinds of dilemmas that they had never had to face before.

Like when some Christians started teaching new converts that it wasn't enough just to be baptized into Jesus. If you really want to be a part of the people of God, then all the male converts need to be circumcised to be saved.

This brought about the church's first ever "business meeting." Luke tells us that "the apostles and elders all met together to consider this."

I know we are separated by a couple of thousand years, but I hope you pick up on the fact that this is going to be an intense meeting. A lot rides on the outcome of this. For two or three years now these people who spent all this time with Jesus have been going around preaching that in Christ there is "neither Jew nor Gentile, slave nor free, male or female."

They have been preaching this idea that God loves everyone. That in Jesus, everyone is invited to join in God's repair of the world.

And now we see what it looks like to have to wrestle with all the implications of such ideas. I love the fact that Luke doesn't cover this up. He lets us see how messy this whole thing was.

But let me see if I can make this clearer for you. I want you to imagine the Christian Pharisees (they are a vibrant part of the first church, and they don't think that following Jesus is a contradiction to Moses!). They believe Jesus is the Messiah, but they are still devout Pharisees.

Actually the Pharisees aren't just jerks. They are passionate about trying to please God. And their main issue in this story is a matter of immense importance to Jewish people in that day—circumcision.

Now I know that some of you have to be thinking, is this really coming up again? I mean, how many times is Acts going to bring this topic up? But for these fellows, this is a lot more than just a surgical procedure.

For them, this is a really big deal. God had given the mark of circumcision to the Israelite people thousands of years earlier. It was God's way of revealing himself as a deeply personal, relational God. It was their centuries-honored sign that they belonged to him.

So these Pharisees stand up and say, "Okay, we aren't giving in on this one." I think on some level they had to be thinking, if we had to do it, so do they. After all, misery loves company.

But Peter and Paul won't hear it.

Peter and Paul and Barnabas have really had their comfort zone demolished. They've gone from being in a nice Jewish isolated world to meeting these people on the outside who don't have the same background but who love God, and whom God loves.

That sounds nice, but it's really, really messy.

These new people in the church don't know who Moses is or what he did. They haven't seen the *Prince of Egypt*. They don't know about Charlton Heston parting the Red Sea. Remember that Pharisees, in order to stay holy, wouldn't even look at women. Some of these new non-Jewish people in the churches probably have gone to visit temple prostitutes. Observant Jews refuse to eat meat with blood in it. These Gentile people like their steak to have a pulse.

At one point in Jewish history, Herod had put a Roman eagle atop their Temple. Thousands of Pharisees protested, and when Roman soldiers threatened to kill them, the Pharisees all lay down and exposed their necks to be axed. As if to say to Herod, if you don't give us this one, then be prepared to commit genocide.

These non-Jewish people grew up going to the market and getting cheaper meat because it had already been sacrificed to idols. It was the Costco of the day.

It was no big deal for the Gentiles to eat meat that was sacrificed to the very images the Pharisees had been willing to die to keep from polluting their holy Temple.

This sounds idealistic, bringing these two dissimilar groups together. It was difficult then, and it's difficult today.

At one point in Acts, it looks as if things could start spinning out of control. But when everything seems to be almost hopeless, they do something that never comes naturally to religious people. They start to compromise.

In this one meeting, they basically chunk over six hundred old commandments, including circumcision. What we are seeing here is the church doing the hard work of wrestling with what it means to be the church in every age and in every context.

There's a Pharisee in All of Us

The Pharisees have taken a bad rap over the past few centuries. We tend to see them as rigid, narrow-minded people who liked to step on kittens. In reality, they were godly people we probably would have liked.

They know the value of tradition. They know that you can cut a tree down in ten minutes, but you can't grow it back in ten years. If you have ever walked into church and not liked some change that has been made, welcome to the club.

There is a Pharisee in all of us.

Now let me hurry to assure you that this passage isn't saying that every new thing a church does is good, and every old thing is bad.

Tradition can be great. There are ancient things that the people of God historically have done that have rich, theological meaning and significance. This passage isn't about throwing all that away.

This passage is about being considerate of the other people and their convictions.

What happens when something that is so meaningful to you is actually not helpful to your brother or sister?

One of the things we should be cautious of is being part of a church that never makes us feel uncomfortable, one that never stretches us but always does things the way we grew up doing them.

What can happen is that we can become so attached to the forms of church, even good forms, maybe especially good forms, that we forget the function of church. We can lose sight of the fact that God is creating a community of people in which there are no walls. Where everyone is welcome.

Which sounds great, but there is a price we must pay for that kind of community.

Just ask the Pharisees in Acts 15.

We tend to focus on the great miracles of Acts, the lame man walking, blind people seeing, people getting healed by shadows and handkerchiefs. But maybe we've been missing some of the most spectacular miracles.

The greatest miracles of all in Acts may not be the healing ones. Think about Peter in Acts 10. For centuries people like Peter have been told not to eat ham and not to hang out with Gentiles. And in one crazy moment God tells him those rules no longer apply.

Or what about Paul? All these years he's believed God is a certain way. He's lived a certain way. And now in the course of one turn on a road to Damascus, everything is changed. Now his life's mission is not to get rid of people but to invite as many people as possible, by whatever means possible, into the Kingdom of God.

This kind of learning and changing has been particularly hard for the fellowship I grew up in. Despite all the great ways that I was taught and shaped by my tribe, one thing I now know about my church tradition (and it's probably just as true of others) is that we don't do change that well.

On the days when I am the most honest, I have to admit that if I had been Peter that day on the tanner's rooftop or in Cornelius' den, I would not have obeyed. I mean, I believe the Bible too much to obey God. When God says he's changing the rules, the proper response is, "You can't do that." Isn't it?

Without doubt, these are some of the greatest miracles of Acts: that people who have done things one way for thousands of years are open to doing it another way for the sake of peace with a brother or sister in Christ. That is an absolute marvel.

It Seems Good to Us

So the church leaders come up with a few rules for helping community to develop between two very different groups of people. They ask for the incoming Gentile believers to do a few things: (1) not eat food polluted by idols, (2) turn from sexual immorality, (3) refrain from eating the meat of strangled animals, and (4) not eat meat with blood. That's it.

The tone here isn't, "You should do this or you won't be saved." The tone of these rules says, "Please help us. If you don't accept these rules, it will make all of our lives a lot harder."

In the course of one meeting, those early leaders of the church give up customs and rituals that have been basic to their faith all of their lives. It has been mandatory for them as Jews to know and honor the stories of Abraham, Jacob and Esau, and Moses. Living just as those great men lived has been the definition of faith for these first Jewish Christians. Now all of that changes. Now they have new rules.

Just four little rules. And I think we can sum up how they accomplished this colossal change by looking at just two verses.

> It seemed good to the Holy Spirit and to us not to burden
> you with anything beyond the following requirements:
> You are to abstain from food sacrificed to idols, from
> blood, from the meat of strangled animals and from
> sexual immorality. You will do well to avoid these things.
> (Acts 15:28–29)

"It seemed good to the Holy Spirit and to us." Think about that phrase, "It seemed good." I sure hope so.

If I had been a Pharisee in the church back then, I think my first reaction to that message would have been, "Come on people, you are discarding just about every rule we learned in Bible school and dealing out legislation on what it means to be the people of God. We want some kind of ironclad regulations, commandments handed down from on high. Give us chapter and verse!"

But what we get is this.[3]

What often happens in our world is that we trick ourselves into such certainty. On more than one occasion I've had people disagree with me over inconsequential church matters, and they (or, if I'm being honest, I) have said something like, "This isn't just my position. This is Jesus' view of things, too." The ultimate trump card.

For some of us, this might be a bit disconcerting.

From the greatest leaders of the earliest Christians, you might expect more conviction. But they don't say this is the way it is. They say, about one of the biggest changes made in all of Acts, "It seems good to us."

These leaders aren't sure what the next step is. They are just trying to be faithful to God, even when it is costing them a ton. And behind it all is this open-handed generosity to the other side, and a deep sense of humility

These Spirit-led people have radical convictions that often land them in jail or get them killed. But they also exhibit amazing generosity toward the beliefs of others.

I believe things, and I believe them with deep conviction. But when I read the stories of these earliest Christians and then look at the way we are perceived today, I wonder: where did we go wrong? How did we get to be known as the kind of people who are so arrogant and mean about what we think, when these first Christians were so gentle and kind about what they believed?

Certainty can be a good friend to arrogance.

What would happen if we thought and acted like those leaders in Acts 15? If we approached our church like this? If we approached our marriages, our relationships, like this?

Do you know that the average male drives 276 miles a year while he is lost? And we guys don't call that arrogant; we call it exploring. Far too often we are not able to admit not being certain. It's very difficult for us to hold our convictions with an open hand. Maybe that's what makes community so hard in our culture.

The Gods in Our Image

But do you know what's so heartbreaking about this passage? It's how the chapter ends.[4] The very next story is about Paul and Barnabas separating because of a disagreement. And you can tell from the language here that it isn't a civil disagreement.This whole chapter is about unity—until we get here. Turns out, the very leaders who sought church-wide reconciliation can't do keep it themselves.

It was the kind of argument that only church disagreements can produce. Arguments like this only come when we assume that God is on our side. Surely Luke could have found a less embarrassing way of saying this.

But he didn't.

He lets us see this story—I think as a precaution to Jesus' followers everywhere. It's a snapshot into the human condition. The one thing these great men and women want the most is the very thing they fail to practice themselves. But you don't have to turn to some Bible story to see this. It's in our newspapers, and history books, and most of all our mirrors.

On June 7, 1964, when a group of religious people had gathered at the local Methodist church like always, they were having another one of their get-togethers, and as usual they started with a prayer.

Of course, they prayed. They were God's chosen people, after all, saved by Jesus to bless the world. But on this particular night, someone wrote down their opening prayer. Sam Bowers, their "preacher and leader" opened with prayer. Here's what he said:

> Oh God, our Heavenly Guide, as finite creatures of time and as dependent creatures of Thine, we acknowledge Thee as our sovereign Lord. Permit freedom and the joys thereof to forever reign throughout our land. . . . May the sweet cup of brotherly fraternity ever be ours to enjoy and build within us that kindred spirit which will keep us unified and strong. Engender within us that wisdom kindred to honorable decisions and the godly work. By the power of Thy infinite spirit and the energizing virtue therein, ever keep before us our . . . pledges of righteousness. Bless us now in this assembly that we may honor Thee in all things, we pray in the name of Christ, our blessed Savior. Amen.[5]

And then the members of the Klu Klux Klan said Amen, got up, and started planning how to carry out "God's goal" for white supremacy.

A few years ago I was talking with a man who was a professional conflict mediator, one who had worked with presidents and international government officials. He had helped nations resolve international conflicts bordering on war, but if you asked him who was the hardest assignment, he wouldn't blink an eye before he told you, "That's easy . . . churches."

Do you know when you are the most vulnerable to this, when you are the most susceptible to failing at this? When you are right.

I should know. I'm right a lot. But the problem with being right is that it makes it really hard to live in community.

You know what is even crazier about this story of the first church split in Acts? It's that God uses even this split to accomplish his purposes! Now God has two church-planting teams going out to tell the world that Jesus is Lord.

Here is a snapshot of how big our God is. He can even bend back our stupidity and our stubbornness to suit his purposes.

But, and let's be clear, this still isn't the dream of God.

Wouldn't it be nice to be part of a community of people where God doesn't have to accomplish things in spite of us—but through us?

I am convinced that the first step in learning how to start a riot is learning how to stop one. We have to learn how to stop fussing with each other.

You know what I find most interesting about this whole story? It's these bottom-line requirements: no bloody meat and no meat offered to idols. You'd think if you were going to cut hundreds of laws, these wouldn't be the ones you would retain.

But they kept them because this is about table fellowship! That's why this is such a big deal. They want to be able to break bread with all their brothers and sisters! Even the ones they disagree with!

Everyone Here Speaks Sign Language

In the 1980s, Nora Ellen Groce, a professor at Yale University, spent some time researching a phenomenon in Martha's Vineyard. Because of a high percentage of intermarriage, Martha's Vineyard had a disproportionate number of deaf people. This in itself is interesting, but what was more fascinating was what Groce found as she researched how this community had dealt with this phenomenon.

In most societies, handicapped people are forced to adapt to the lifestyle of those who are not handicapped. But not on Martha's Vineyard. Croce expected to find that those who were deaf had coped by writing things down on paper in order for non-deaf people to understand them. But what she found was fascinating. Instead of the deaf people being reduced to writing everything, the community of people at Martha's Vineyard had all learned sign language!

I love the way Tim Keller talks about this:

> Indeed, what had happened was that an entire community had disadvantaged itself *en masse* for the sake of a minority. Instead of making the non-hearing minority learn to read lips, the whole hearing majority learned signing. . . . They changed their culture in order to include an otherwise disadvantaged minority but in the process made themselves and their society richer.[6]

We have no idea what kind of sacrifices those earliest Christians made. It's hard for us to imagine the pain of a slave and slave master sitting down at the same table. It's hard to imagine how difficult it would be for a Jew and a Gentile to dine side by side. In that culture men and women also did not eat together.

But, one at a time, each barrier was knocked down!

It's hard to imagine sacrifices like those, but it's not hard to imagine what it would look like today. Chances are that you have some people in your church you don't like, and they don't like you. Chances are someone in your church has wronged you and sinned against you. I imagine their faces are coming to mind right now. If not, rest assured, your face is coming to their mind!

One option for you is to just go with the flow. No one will be surprised if you just subtly ignore those folks or maybe slip a rumor you've heard about them into the ever-moving gossip mill. Probably none of your associates will realize that what you are doing is going against the grain of the gospel, but you will.

If we want our discipleship to be anything like that in the early church, then we've got to take their sacrifices seriously. We've got to take the table of communion seriously.

Loving others and giving up whatever we have to surrender in order to include them in our faith family is at the heart of what it means to be a Christian and to participate in the Lord's Supper. In this community of the Lord, no one is a second-class citizen. Everyone can have a seat. Enemies and friends, Jews and Gentiles, male and female.

This table is big enough for everyone because it is a table prepared by Jesus.

Chapter 12

The Risk
of Security

"If the safest place to be is the center of God's will, how do you explain . . . why is it that the biblical word for witness is actually the word for martyrs?"

—Erwin McManus

"Optimism is for Hallmark, not for a community that worships a crucified God. When optimism is the church's business, then we allow it to screen us from seeing reality. The church is not in the business of optimism and positivity but of trust in a new reality that will be born within this broken one."

—Andrew Root[1]

It's tough to talk about the possibility of dying at the Olive Garden. Maybe it's because of the breadsticks, or because everything just seems so nice. It just feels off somehow. A few years ago, Leslie and I had lunch with the resident missionary couple at our church.

They were headed to a destination in north Africa that I can't write about here for security reasons, but chances are you've heard about this place. George Clooney is a big fan.

She is an ethnomusicologist; he is a community development guru. Their working plan is that when they leave a place, people there will have clean water, better returns on their harvests, and songs, poems, and stories about meeting Jesus. Which sounds pretty good to me.

So it was strange that, sitting there in Olive Garden, they were talking about what to do if their village or home were to be attacked by hostile militants. Leslie and I were leaning in, trying to understand why these dear people have chosen to take their little family and put them in harm's way. And that's when they told us.

"Jesus said to go into all the world. He never said anything about coming back."

Good point.

One of the best ways to see what is important to any culture is to look at the language people use to describe and categorize the reality around them. The more words that we use to talk about something, the more important it is. So it's not surprising to realize that the English language has over a hundred words or phrases to talk about money. We call it "cash, greenbacks, Benjamins," etc. Because money is obviously something that we think is important enough to refer to repeatedly.

But money does not have the most words. The idea that has captured more of our imagination than almost anything else in the English language is death. We have over two hundred ways to talk about death. We say someone, "Passed away, kicked the bucket, bought the farm, or assumed room temperature."

Our lives are oriented around death. Because ever since death entered the world, our primary concern has been about how to avoid it.

Do You Believe in Magic?

Nobody wants to come to the end of their days and find that they never really lived. But the irony is that, while most of us want to have lived all the days of our lives, we tend to make decisions that aren't oriented around that.

We make decisions, instead, that are aimed at minimizing risk. This is true even in our churches. Maybe especially in our churches.

Think about the prayer requests we hear in our churches, Bible classes, and small groups. If we tried to figure out what Christians in our country think is important based on what we are asked to pray for, you most certainly would conclude that physical health is the most important thing in the world to people of faith.

I find this fascinating, because I grew up thinking that one of the goals of Christians today should be to live like the early Christians. Especially like the Christians in the book of Acts. But those Christians didn't pray like we do.

When we were in Ephesus and Corinth a few years ago, we saw votive artifacts from people who prayed to their gods for healing. They would pray and pay to whatever god they thought might listen, and then they would leave a clay artifact shaped like the body part they wanted healed.

They would do these rituals, overwhelmingly, for healing.

We pray today much like the ancient pagans used magic.

In the ancient world, magic was seen as a way of coercing the forces that run this world to act on your behalf. And the city of Ephesus was a hub of this kind of thinking about the gods.

Ephesus is a center of magical power, as well as religious and political power. So, when the gospel gets to Ephesus, we can expect some serious conflict with this kind of power. Like this story Luke shares:

God did extraordinary miracles through Paul, so that even handkerchiefs and aprons that had touched him were taken to the sick, and their illnesses were cured and the evil spirits left them.

Some Jews who went around driving out evil spirits tried to invoke the name of the Lord Jesus over those who were demon-possessed. They would say, "In the name of Jesus, whom Paul preaches, I command you to come out." Seven sons of Sceva, a Jewish chief priest, were doing this. [One day] the evil spirit answered them, "Jesus I know, and I know about Paul, but who are you?" Then the man who had the evil spirit jumped on them and overpowered them all. He gave them such a beating that they ran out of the house naked and bleeding. (Acts 19:11–16)

What a great story! "Jesus we know about, and Paul we've heard of, but who in the world are you?" This is brilliant! I picture the demon in his best Robert De Niro voice basically saying, "Are you talking to me?"

I know that on some level we've got to be thinking, what just happened? But the point of this story is clear. Jesus isn't magic. In Paul's day each person tried to use the most powerful deity they knew. They would invoke that god's name over other pseudo-gods.

But this Jesus story doesn't work like that.

C. S. Lewis points out that magic is an attempt to gain power without having to pay the price of humble submission to the god you are invoking.

But Jesus doesn't work like Zeus. The gospel has power, but it is not magic.

Jesus is Lord of all the earth, but he's not some god that can be manipulated or coerced. And that is a good thing for us to remember.

In a world where Jesus' name is used to justify everything from pick-eting funerals of homosexuals to selling bumper stickers or voting for some candidate, it's good to be reminded that Jesus doesn't just endorse our agendas.

He's bigger than we are. And his name can't be used to manipu-late demons or keep our team from fumbling. Look at what happens when the people hear about this.

The Bonfire of Ephesus

This is a beautiful story of repentance that is starting to happen all over Ephesus. People are starting to realize that the one true God is not a God whose power can be co-opted just by saying the right words or wearing the right amulet.

> When this became known to the Jews and Greeks living in Ephesus, they were all seized with fear, and the name of the Lord Jesus was held in high honor. Many of those who believed now came and openly confessed their evil deeds. A number who had practiced sorcery brought their scrolls together and burned them publicly. When they calculated the value of the scrolls, the total came to fifty thousand drachmas. In this way the word of the Lord spread widely and grew in power. (Acts 19:17–20)

My guess is that the story of Sceva's sons getting thrashed by an upset demoniac spreads like wildfire. Those pompous (and incompetent) exorcists become the talk of the town. Not only are these sorcerers and their patron gods embarrassed. Far more important, the stories about Jesus began to spread.

As people learn more about the Christ preached by Paul, a large number of the Ephesians turn their backs on magic and this entire way of relating to deity. People all over the region began turning to

Jesus. Since most of the people in that pagan capital had trusted in the pagan gods of that day, this repentance involves their public renunciation of the magic charms and incantations linked to those other gods.

So they have a bonfire revival. They get all their magic books and build a huge, public fire. Actually, these "books" probably are scrolls. Most people in their world can't afford scrolls, so owning one is a luxury. The magic books burned here are especially valuable.

These are books that come with a promise that you can control a small part of your world. They are recipes and formulas written as a way of manipulating the principalities and powers that people believed ran the world. They involved the ability to make people fall in love, or to put death curses on a friend who betrayed you. Which is a bit darker than a Harry Potter book.

Common sense would tell them to sell the books if they don't believe them anymore.

But what we see here is not common sense. This is repentance. And what these converts are doing here is significant, because in these days when book burnings happen, they are always done by the rulers.

So what we see here is a bunch of people who aren't kings or queens or emperors who are publicly revolting against this way of relating to God. They're doing this because they no longer believe God is like that. And it costs them.

The money amount here is the modern equivalent of three to four million dollars. So this is a beautiful, captivating story of what repentance looks like. But, as beautiful as this story may be, there is a victim. Because behind every book burning is a very angry publisher.

So it is important that this story ends by letting us know how much these books cost. As much money as this is, some of these people know it's just a drop in the bucket compared to what's to come.

Some really smart people see the handwriting on the wall. They know that their economy is based on the ideas going up in flames in that bonfire. And whenever you see people burning money, you can be sure that a riot is not far off.

> About that time there arose a great disturbance about the Way. A silversmith named Demetrius, who made silver shrines of Artemis, brought in no little business for the craftsmen. He called them together, along with the workmen in related trades, and said: "Men, you know we receive a good income from this business. And you see and hear how this fellow Paul has convinced and led astray large numbers of people here in Ephesus and in practically the whole province of Asia. He says that man-made gods are no gods at all. There is danger not only that our trade will lose its good name, but also that the temple of the great goddess Artemis will be discredited, and the goddess herself, who is worshiped throughout the province of Asia and the world, will be robbed of her divine majesty." (Acts 19:23–27)

As soon as we are introduced to Demetrius we find out that he has an agenda. He's a silversmith who makes shrines of Artemis. Artemis was known as a fertility god, but she was so much more than that. She was the most popular of all the Greek goddesses, known for protecting women in childbirth. And that was a big deal because a large percentage of birthing mothers died then.

Artemis is the goddess for the moms out there. But Artemis has a dark side. Legend tells us Artemis has permission from Zeus to kill whatever children she wants to at childbirth. So the people want to keep Artemis happy.

But it doesn't take a theologian to recognize there are other motives in Demetrius' speech. Demetrius is concerned about protecting his booming business. He and his silversmith buddies operate the Sam's Club of Artemis-related products. And this preacher named Paul is becoming a burr under his saddle blanket.

Demetrius' main problem when we meet him is what Paul has been saying around town about idols—namely that "human-made gods are no gods at all."

That phrase stings a bit if you are a man who makes gods for a living.

Look at what this upset silversmith says. "There is danger that Artemis herself will lose her good name," he warns. Now it doesn't take a serious Bible scholar to realize that this really is not Demetrius' concern.

If making statues of Jesus would have made this man more money, he and his fellow artisans would have converted with the rest of their neighbors. They work for the system, and the system works for them.

And they certainly don't need some punk Christian coming in and saying that the idols they craft are just decorative, powerless trinkets.

His real god isn't Artemis. His god is his wallet. And he isn't alone. The entire city of Ephesus begins to unravel:

> When they heard this, they were furious and began
> shouting: "Great is Artemis of the Ephesians!" Soon the
> whole city was in an uproar. The people seized Gaius
> and Aristarchus, Paul's traveling companions from
> Macedonia, and rushed as one man into the theater. Paul

wanted to appear before the crowd, but the disciples would not let him. Even some of the officials of the province, friends of Paul, sent him a message begging him not to venture into the theater.

The assembly was in confusion: Some were shouting one thing, some another. Most of the people did not even know why they were there. The Jews pushed Alexander to the front, and some of the crowd shouted instructions to him. He motioned for silence in order to make a defense before the people. But when they realized he was a Jew, they all shouted in unison for about two hours: "Great is Artemis of the Ephesians!" (Acts 19:28–34)

I love that Luke tells us some people don't even know why they are there. Some people are yelling one thing and some people another, and there is some guy in the middle of this who hasn't got a clue what's going on.

This is mass pandemonium. Mob mentality at its best.

This huge amphitheater in Ephesus is able to hold about twenty-five thousand people. And it is designed with precision. You can sit at the very top of this theater, and if someone in the middle drops a pin, you can hear it.

So the noise of the mob that day is overpowering.

Maybe you've been to a college football game and seen this kind of passion, or maybe you've been shopping on Black Friday and sensed this kind of mob mentality. Or maybe you've gone to a political rally and witnessed this kind of anger.

Many of us have seen crowd excitement like this. Some of us have even been a part of such an upheaval. And I think that's important to pay attention to. It is an indication of what we riot over, isn't it?

It's easy for us to hear this story and assume that it's some distant story from the past. But it is a snapshot of how we still do it today. We riot over the pettiest things, don't we? Do you want to know what your little god is? Find out what you will riot for.

In the middle of all this, Paul tries to get in to talk to the screaming mob. Which, let's be honest, is crazy. All of his friends that day tell him so.

Thousands of people in that amphitheater want to rip him to pieces, and Paul thinks he can talk sense into them. That's nutty. Cooler heads have to convince "the little apostle" to stay out of there.

Finally the city clerk comes in and quiets down the crowd.

> The city clerk quieted the crowd and said: "Men of Ephesus, doesn't all the world know that the city of Ephesus is the guardian of the temple of the great Artemis and of her image, which fell from heaven? Therefore, since these facts are undeniable, you ought to be quiet and not do anything rash. You have brought these men here, though they have neither robbed temples nor blasphemed our goddess. If, then, Demetrius and his fellow craftsmen have a grievance against anybody, the courts are open and there are proconsuls. They can press charges. If there is anything further you want to bring up, it must be settled in a legal assembly. As it is, we are in danger of being charged with rioting because of today's events. In that case we would not be able to account for this commotion, since there is no reason for it." After he had said this, he dismissed the assembly. (Acts 19:35–41)

He comes in and recites the propaganda for Artemis. He tells a story about Artemis that everyone knows. All of them have heard the legend that Artemis' image fell from heaven.

What probably happened is that a meteorite fell in Ephesus, and people saw in it something that looked to them like a woman. So this entire religion was based around this meteor rock.

The city clerk is just standing up there and reminding the rioters of Artemis propaganda they already know.

On a side note, I want you to notice what the man says about Paul. He says Paul has "neither robbed temples nor blasphemed our goddess." Paul hasn't gone into this culture just to attack their gods. He has come in and preached about what God is up to in Jesus, and it works. In a pluralistic society, you and I need to learn how to talk *about* Jesus—not *against* Mohammed or Buddha.

The way you and I live will speak a lot more than what we say. Paul's way of following Jesus is a message the Ephesians cannot ignore, because he is living in a dramatically different way than they.

Risky Business

I know that this particular story in Acts sounds like some ancient, primitive religious thing that would never happen to us.

But one more thing about the goddess Artemis. The name Artemis is based on the root Greek word for safety or health.

Artemis sounds like some ancient deity, but the truth is she is worshiped by millions every day. And standing juxtaposed against this mob chanting for health and safety but acting dangerously is this guy named Paul, who wants to go into an assembly that has gathered to kill him. Everyone else there is out of his mind wanting security, but Paul is willing to risk everything.

Because Paul doesn't worship Artemis.

I remember the day I was able to go to this amphitheater. We were visiting Ephesus, and the last day we were there, they took us to this historic place that has been incredibly well preserved.

We stood in this massive coliseum where you can hear whispers no matter where you are standing, and I imagined the mob that day. Then our tour guide showed us this little side room where people who needed to hide could hunker down. It was a room created for days when the crowd didn't like the message or if the play wasn't popular. It was a hideout where the actor or speaker who was the target of their wrath could retreat to safety.

Our guide told us there was a good chance this is where Paul was while the riot was going on. I remember having a profound moment there when I realized that this was my story.

It's a story that refuses to bow its knee to the god of security or to be reduced to just making people nice.

The way of Jesus is diametrically opposed to civil religions, even ones that bear his name. Maybe especially ones that wear his name.

A few years ago, the historian Andrew Wells gave an interview in which he spoke about how the Christian religion was different from other major religions. He noted that every other world religion's epicenter, its strongest point of influence, is where that religion began. Buddhism began in the Far East, and that's still where it is the strongest. Islam started in the Middle East, and that is still its major hub.

But this doesn't hold true for Christianity. In fact, Wells pointed out that today there are more Christians in Africa than anywhere else. And then Wells said something fascinating. He said that Christianity has a center that is always moving. The Jesus movement began in Jerusalem and then went to the Greeks, then to North Africa and Rome and England and America.

Christianity's center is always on the move. What is particularly interesting is why it is moving. Andrew Wells says it's because "I think that there is a certain vulnerability, a fragility, at the heart of Christianity. You might say that this is the vulnerability of the cross."[2]

In other words, what has happened throughout human history is that Christianity has gone into places through vulnerable self-sacrifice, but over time it becomes domesticated. Over time what it means to become a Christian becomes muted and safe. We begin to develop ways of being Christian that are "safe and fun for the whole family."

And when that happens, according to Wells, the center of Christianity just moves on.

I have noticed over the past few months something about human nature, including my own. The one thing that will reduce us to our basest instinct is this desire to be secure or healthy. Watch any news channel these days and you will see that when we talk about security or health, people automatically become belligerent, rude, and sometimes hateful. These subjects push our buttons.

Almost, at times, like a riot.

But that's not our story.

Erwin McManus says it well: "Jesus' death wasn't to free us from dying, but to free us from the fear of death. Jesus came to liberate us so that we could die up front and then live. Jesus Christ wants to take us to places where only dead men and women can go."[3]

That is what our brave missionary friends were trying to get at that day in Olive Garden. They knew that if they were going to belong to a story bigger than themselves, they were going to have to orient their lives around something more than their death. They were taking their place in the long line of followers of Jesus who have gone against the dominant impulses of our culture for self-preservation. Because the way of Jesus is not the way of Artemis.

Because the real risk of security is that you might be worshiping a god who is no god at all.

Chapter 13

Snakebites and **Shipwrecks**

"Lord of the wind and the waves, take us, your servants to where you will."

—A prayer Celtic missionaries would pray after setting sail for unknown territory[1]

"An adventure is only an inconvenience rightly considered. An inconvenience is an adventure wrongly considered."

—G .K. Chesterton

In the beginning, before God ever got fully into the business of creating light and oak trees and butterflies, Genesis tells us that God's Spirit hovered above the water. That might sound incidental, but to a Hebrew it meant something.

To the Hebrew mind, the sea was not just a good vacationing spot. It was something to be feared. To the Hebrew mind, the sea was the abyss. Some people think that an average Jew back then didn't know how to swim. Jewish people as a whole were not a seafaring race. They left yacht racing to the other nations.

So it is significant that the Jewish creation story starts off with the Spirit of God hovering over the deep. This was the moment when

God tamed the chaos of the deep. When God had brought order to the void.

And everything was just fine until . . .

Adam and Eve channeled their inner Dr. Doolittle and had a conversation with a snake.

And, as a result, all of creation fell into disarray. Genesis tells us that now thorns and thistles infected the world God had just made. Thorns and thistles refers to more than just farming problems. It is a nod to tsunamis and earthquakes and volcanoes. The world is now fundamentally broken . . . and in just a few chapters we find that now the world has flooded.

The sea became dangerous again.

If you think about it, most of the really scary stories, the "Saw I-V" of the Old Testament, involve the sea. Daniel has a vision of beasts coming up out of the sea. The Jews thought of the sea like I grew up thinking of Freddy Krueger.

It was a monster.

The only reason they would ever go out on the ocean was if they really trusted God, or if, like Jonah, they really didn't.

Because to them, it was more than just a body of water; it was a fallen cosmic power.

That's why Revelation tells us that when heaven comes to earth, there will be no more sea. This is why when God comes to Job to show him how powerful he is, one of the things he tells Job is about his power over the sea.[2]

Throughout ancient Hebrew literature, the sea appears as a primitive cosmic force that, if not held in check, could submerge the world and return it to chaos. But think back for a moment to this whole Garden of Eden business.

If, for the Jewish person, the sea was a symbol for evil, then the snake was even more so. Whole cults in the ancient world were built around the power of the serpent.

It's interesting that while the brunt of the responsibility for disobeying God goes to Adam and Eve, the snake doesn't get off scot-free.

> So the LORD God said to the serpent, "Because you have
> done this,
>
> > "Cursed are you above all the livestock
> > > and all the wild animals!
> > You will crawl on your belly
> > > and you will eat dust
> > > all the days of your life.
> > And I will put enmity
> > > between you and the woman,
> > > and between your offspring and hers;
> > he will crush your head,
> > > and you will strike his heel." (Gen. 3:14–15)

Now if you are Eve, you've got to be thinking, "That's it? I get childbirth and the snake gets its legs taken away?" (In the words of Bill Cosby, if you ever think childbirth is easy, just take your bottom lip and pull it over your head.) Eve has got to be thinking that the snake got off easy.

After the Fall, the entire universe has changed; all creation is now in rebellion' including the sea. So they will stay away from it.

But have you noticed that throughout Acts Paul is on a boat? And furthermore, every boat seems to wreck whenever he's on board. If you are a sea captain, you've got to be thinking that Paul isn't the best passenger to invite onto your ship. His name should be high on TSA's list.

What's even more shocking is that Paul still wants to go! If you were just reading this story for the first time, you would expect Paul to be the John Madden of boat trips, but he's not.

In the next to last chapter of Acts, Paul has been in prison for two years at this point for crimes he didn't commit. He's been passed from one court to the next. Finally, to escape an assassination, he appeals to Caesar's court.

So now he's on his way to Rome. On a boat again, in a storm, and this happens:

> On the fourteenth night we were still being driven across the Adriatic Sea, when about midnight the sailors sensed they were approaching land. They took soundings and found that the water was a hundred and twenty feet deep. A short time later they took soundings again and found it was ninety feet deep. Fearing that we would be dashed against the rocks, they dropped four anchors from the stern and prayed for daylight. In an attempt to escape from the ship, the sailors let the lifeboat down into the sea, pretending they were going to lower some anchors from the bow. Then Paul said to the centurion and the soldiers, "Unless these men stay with the ship, you cannot be saved." So the soldiers cut the ropes that held the lifeboat and let it fall away.
>
> Just before dawn Paul urged them all to eat. "For the last fourteen days," he said, "you have been in constant suspense and have gone without food—you haven't eaten anything. Now I urge you to take some food. You need it to survive. Not one of you will lose a single hair from his

head." After he said this, he took some bread and gave thanks to God in front of them all. Then he broke it and began to eat. They were all encouraged and ate some food themselves. Altogether there were 276 of us on board. When they had eaten as much as they wanted, they lightened the ship by throwing the grain into the sea.

When daylight came, they did not recognize the land, but they saw a bay with a sandy beach, where they decided to run the ship aground if they could. Cutting loose the anchors, they left them in the sea and at the same time untied the ropes that held the rudders. Then they hoisted the foresail to the wind and made for the beach. But the ship struck a sandbar and ran aground. The bow stuck fast and would not move, and the stern was broken to pieces by the pounding of the surf.

The soldiers planned to kill the prisoners to prevent any of them from swimming away and escaping. But the centurion wanted to spare Paul's life and kept them from carrying out their plan. He ordered those who could swim to jump overboard first and get to land. The rest were to get there on planks or on pieces of the ship. In this way everyone reached land in safety. (Acts 27:27–44)

It sounds a bit weird for Paul to give a pep talk right in the middle of a typhoon. Luke's earliest readers might have thought it even stranger than we do. When folks in the ancient world told stories, the main character would talk. But in shipwreck stories, the hero would always pour out laments or woes.

Not this time. Paul, in the middle of a storm that has been raging for fourteen days, stands up and starts talking like he's Tony Robbins. "Everything is going to turn out fine," he assures his shipmates. "Don't worry. Sure we're going to have a small shipwreck, but don't worry. You'll be okay."

And he is right.

The Island of Malta

They survive the storm, and they wash up on an island named Malta. But they don't know the name of the island until they get there. It's not like they were aiming for it. They had been drifting without a compass for two weeks.

> Once safely on shore, we found out that the island was called Malta. The islanders showed us unusual kindness. They built a fire and welcomed us all because it was raining and cold. Paul gathered a pile of brushwood and, as he put it on the fire, a viper, driven out by the heat, fastened itself on his hand. When the islanders saw the snake hanging from his hand, they said to each other, "This man must be a murderer; for though he escaped from the sea, Justice has not allowed him to live." But Paul shook the snake off into the fire and suffered no ill effects. The people expected him to swell up or suddenly fall dead, but after waiting a long time and seeing nothing unusual happen to him, they changed their minds and said he was a god. (Acts 28:1–6)

The sailors have done everything they know to do to keep their ship headed roughly north toward the coast of Europe. To the south on the African coast lies a fate they don't even want to imagine. On the Barbary Coast, tribes of pirates make their living by salvaging the cargo of ships wrecked on their shore.

Worse than that, among these tribes are bands of cannibals, whose chief diet is the people who wash up on their shore.

All of Paul's shipwrecked companions know what would happen to them if the storm drives their ship too far south. . . . And we complain when our flight's delayed. But they're not in the clear yet; at least Paul's not.

Trouble seems to track Paul. He gets out of the water and into the fire. Or, at least, almost into it. He's helping to keep his shipmates warm when a viper clinging to a stick latches onto Paul's hand. In the ancient world, when someone comes right out of a shipwreck only to immediately get bitten by a snake, this would be seen as bad luck. Some things never change.

Some of the islanders think the snakebite is a sure sign that the gods have judged this man. Someone (we can only assume it was Pat Robertson's great-great-granddad) points out that this surely must mean that Paul is guilty of doing something bad.

Remember, snakes had special meaning. They were seen as more than animals. They were symbolic of the powers that run this world, so people were terrified of them. Which may be exactly why Luke is telling us all of this.

The sea and the snake were classic symbols of evil. And now at the final moment, it seems as though the dark powers are about to do Paul in. Mediterranean vipers are deadly. Almost instantly so. People who get bitten by one seldom walk it off. But Paul does.

Luke is telling us again that the world is being set right in Jesus and his followers. But don't expect this to mean we won't have times when the snake bites or the ship wrecks. The Lord does not exempt us from troubles. He helps us during times of trouble.

Over the past few years, I have become more and more sensitive to the "sales pitch" that Christians give new people who are thinking about joining the Jesus movement. We love to talk about the pros— all the reasons to sign on as a disciple. Follow Jesus to find peace.

Follow Jesus to receive freedom from shame and condemnation. Follow Jesus and you'll have the resources to forgive.

All of which are true and good things, but let's not forget that there are lots of good reasons *not* to follow Jesus.

Even Jesus thinks so. He warns everyone who is interested in following him to consider the cost of discipleship. Because to follow Jesus means to pick up a cross.

Sometimes I wonder if we are so set on getting people to make decisions that we forget to make disciples. Sometimes I wonder if we've forgotten to tell people that life with God has its storms. Life with Jesus can get pretty bumpy.

One theologian recently pointed out something I had never considered before. He suggests that Luke is purposefully trying to parallel the end of Acts with the end of his Gospel. Specifically the crucifixion and resurrection.

What had happened to Jesus is now happening to his followers. If the sea is a symbol for the abyss, for darkness and death, then Paul was about to be swallowed up by it. But a few days later he walks away. *Because the sea doesn't have a storm big enough to swallow Easter.*

Because when the storms and snakes have done their worst, when they have exhausted their power, Jesus is still bigger.

Publius Meets Paul

That is what's so great about how this story ends.

There was an estate nearby that belonged to Publius, the chief official of the island. He welcomed us to his home and for three days entertained us hospitably. His father was sick in bed, suffering from fever and dysentery. Paul went in to see him and, after prayer, placed his hands on him and healed him. When this had happened, the rest of the sick on the island came and were cured. They honored us in many ways and when we were ready to sail, they furnished us with the supplies we needed. (Acts 28:7–10)

Paul winds up meeting Publius, who is the chief official on the island, and Paul heals his father.

Now, let me state the obvious.

This meeting never should have happened. If Paul had enjoyed a smooth cruise and gone straight to Rome, he never would have met Publius. To take this one step farther, how could Paul ever have planned this meeting?

It took a shipwreck for Paul to get onto this island.

And once he's there, if Paul had tried to arrange a meeting with this guy, he probably would have been laughed at. Publius is an important, wealthy man; Paul is a convict on death row. But Paul has just been bitten by a snake and survived it, so he's a bit of a local celebrity now.

This chapter of Acts starts off looking like a total disaster. But, as Mark Batterson points out in his book *Wild Goose Chase*, God is working behind the scenes—in this case through shipwrecks and snakebites.

Before leaving this story, we should notice that the conversion of the inhabitants of Malta, from the governor all the way down to the most nondescript peasant, is not accomplished by preaching. The Maltese are drawn to Jesus because the followers of Jesus acted like Jesus.

It is also worth noting that the people who washed up on this island hungry, wet, cold, and in desperate need of aid turn out to be the aid-givers. The tables quickly turn when Paul begins to heal the sick. Here we find Paul and the other shipwrecked Jesus followers giving a glimpse into what the Lord has wanted his church to look like in every age in every place.

Sociologist Rodney Stark has pointed out that one of the primary reasons for the spread of the Jesus movement was the way Christians responded to the sick.

During the reign of Marcus Aurelius around A.D. 165, there was an epidemic of what may have been smallpox that killed between a third to a fourth of the population. Less than a century later, there was another epidemic in which five thousand people died every day in the city of Rome alone.

People, as you might expect, panicked. Instinctively, people stayed away from people who were dying, so most people died alone with no one to care for them. Christians were different. Christians remembered the stories of Jesus touching and healing lepers.

Dionysius, a third-century bishop of Alexandria, wrote about the Christians' actions: "Heedless of the danger, they took charge of the sick, attending to their every need, and ministering to them in Christ. And with them departed this life serenely happy, for they were infected by others with the disease, drawing on themselves the sickness of their neighbors, and cheerfully accepting their pains."[3]

Governor Publius is not a theologian. He doesn't know about David or Ruth. But even this Gentile knows that life is filled with sickness and pain and death. This is the inescapable lot of every human.

So, when Publius sees his father made whole by the power of Jesus, he has to be impressed with this undeniable demonstration that Jesus is stronger than all the forces of evil that cause human suffering. He may not understand it yet in theological terms, but Publius has just witnessed the gospel truth that the curse that has hung over humanity for thousands of years is being lifted. And now, he and all his subjects understandably want to know about Jesus.

Publius' story reminds us again that the evil powers that seem to have run the cosmos for centuries have been put on notice. Now nothing can stop the redemptive movement of God through his people.

The Maps Are the Best Part

To me, one of the best parts of my Bible is the maps. Technically, they're not even in the Bible. Publishers just decided to throw them in there.

Have you ever paid attention to those things?

Just try following all the Christians traveling through Acts. Their routes make it look as if their travel agent was a fourth-grader with ADHD. Paul goes on three missionary journeys, and from our point of view the route for none of them really makes sense.

On his first trip, he leaves Antioch, sails to the island of Cyprus, crosses the island on foot, sails to Paphos, climbs the interior mountains to Pisidian Antioch, gets chased down the road to Iconium, then to Lystra (where they stone Paul), and finally to Derbe. Then he backtracks right back through all the places he has just been run out of.

Following Paul's journeys is just about as difficult as following some of his letters.

On his second trip he takes the super highway from Antioch to the high-mountain churches in the territory we call eastern Turkey today. Then Paul heads to Asia, toward Ephesus, the largest city in that region, but God says, "No, Paul, not there." So Paul turns north and aims at Bithynia, and again God stops him.

In one of the strangest verses in the Bible, Luke says the Holy Spirit won't let him go in. As if God is the bouncer for Bithynia. So Paul takes the only road God leaves open and winds up in Troas, where he preaches about Jesus.

This is where Dr. Luke, the guy who goes on to become the author of Acts, joins him. Together, they catch a boat to Philippi, because of a vision they have in which a man from Macedonia invites them to "Come over and help us."

Little does Paul know that he was accepting an invitation to get beaten bloody and spend a night in jail. But at this point in the story, we begin to realize even that wouldn't have stopped him.

At every stop along the way, Paul introduces people to the compelling story of Jesus. But in almost every town he visits, he encounters extreme opposition. In Thessalonica, some of the Jewish leaders stir up big trouble for him. He tries moving south to the next town, Berea, but the troublemakers find out he's there and come to deal more misery to him. So Paul has to run away to Athens.

Without the maps, it would be almost impossible to keep up with how they did this. In a world where most people never travelled past thirty miles of their birthplace, it takes the resurrection of Jesus for us to understand why they did it.

While Paul is in that ancient capital of philosophy, he finds himself preaching to people who are the exact opposite of the kind of people he thought he'd be preaching to.

They're not Jewish. Here in Athens they're pagan Greeks.

Look at what Paul tells them:

The God who made the world and everything in it is the
Lord of heaven and earth and does not live in temples
built by hands. And he is not served by human hands, as if
he needed anything, because he himself gives all men life
and breath and everything else. From one man he made
every nation of men, that they should inhabit the whole
earth; and he determined the times set for them and the
exact places where they should live. God did this so that

men would seek him and perhaps reach out for him and find him, though he is not far from each one of us. (Acts 17:24–27)

Here's a guy who earlier in his life thought he had his career charted. He probably had goals set, plans made, that would take him exactly where he wanted to be in three decades. He was on track to be a big deal.

Now his entire life has been turned upside down. He looks like he's out of control. And Paul tells these people that God has ordained the times and places that we would live.

He tells the Athenians that God is so big, so huge that he controls the destiny of nations, and of the universe. He is bringing chaos to order. He tells them God has a purpose for them living where they are living and when.

Part of God's purpose is that they might come to know the Lord. Paul's point is that this Jesus isn't just another god in their panoply. He's not just another deity they should try to keep happy; Jesus is, in fact, the image of the very God that their lives are already oriented around, even if they are unaware of it.

The very reason that they were born in this time and this place was because God was trying to draw all parts of creation back to himself. And that's true from Stoic philosophers in first-century Athens to soccer moms twenty-one centuries later.

Now that's not to say that all of life is already determined. In fact, Acts seems to suggest an opposite view. That's both the horror and the adventure of it.

Radical open-endedness has always characterized the human experience.

There's been a real movement in the last couple of decades to emphasize life as a story. And I like that, but the problem is that we try to make it into a certain kind of story. No one wants to live in a tragedy. But we don't get to choose the story that will make up what we call a life.

Our stories aren't always going to turn out perfectly.

I have a friend named Grant who was a rising star in the sports television industry. He was regularly a commentator on national television for sporting events at the highest level. Until he was betrayed by a few of his co-workers and friends. They undercut him because they wanted to get his job. This would be devastating to anyone, but looking back on it my friend says, "The most powerful witness I gave in my years at that particular sports network wasn't an explanation of God's existence or some particular doctrine. It was forgiving those friends who betrayed me." He said, "I'd get fired everyday if it meant having the chance to forgive."

Which is not something people normally say.

A few years ago, Beth, one of my friends from church, was diagnosed with advanced breast cancer. It was a crushing blow to her little family, especially since they had just recently gone through another loss. Beth entered an aggressive form of chemo, and her family pulled together to savor whatever time they had left with their mom.

Eventually the chemo worked, and Beth's life is back to normal. But I'll never forget what Beth and her family said during the darkest days. She said, "I've never been closer to my family or friends than I am right now. . . . I'd have gotten cancer sooner if I'd have known how much God would bless me through it."

This was before she heard she was in remission.

I'm not suggesting that losing your job is good, or that God sends cancer to people as a way to bless them. There are too many awful Christian clichés out there about "God needing another angel," and I don't want to add to that.

The point of this story isn't that there is a reason for everything, but that God is so good he *brings reason to everything.*

The truth is our lives are going to have a million different left turns. They will involve tragedies and adventure, heartbreak and loss, joy and despair. And the temptation during the hard times always has been to give in to the belief that the universe is just a cold, dark place. All of us at some point face the temptation to believe that all hope is lost.

But what the early Christians discovered is that our lives are no longer oriented around the snakebites or the shipwrecks.

Because new creation is breaking out, and the powers of evil cannot stop it.

If we really believe in Jesus, we aren't superstitious. We aren't even a little *stitious.*

To use God's first metaphor to describe Jesus' victory: Satan may have bruised Christ's heel, but Jesus has crushed the snake's head. As folks on Malta could see with their own eyes, a new world is already breaking out among us.

Jesus is drawing all things back to himself. He stands above our mini-stories and is drawing them back into his grand, ongoing story.

All of us enjoy a book with a good ending. This story of Jesus just happens to have the best ending ever. I like the way Andrew Root says this:

> *Death is not the church's obsession; no, the church's obses-sion is God and God's future,* a future where death is no more, where death that has been insidiously grafted within our structures is destroyed, where the hungry are fed, the oppressed find freedom, and the sick are healed. The church exists in death, for if it doesn't, it has no footing in reality; but standing in death the church lives and acts for the future.[4]

In life, sometime there are shipwrecks, and sometimes snake bites. But these catastrophes no longer have the last word. They don't even have the main word. Because God is so big that he's able to take these open-ended stories and draw them back to himself.

He's redeeming all of it.

Even the shipwrecks and snakebites.

Chapter 14

Unleashed

"Here is the world. Beautiful and terrible things will happen. Don't be afraid."

　—Frederick Buechner[1]

"Everything dies, baby, that's a fact, but maybe everything that dies someday comes back."

　—Bruce Springsteen

On the triumphal Arch of Titus in the Forum at Rome, we can see a carving of Titus ascending to heaven. In the opening scene of Acts, we find Jesus doing the same thing.

Over the past few years, people have speculated about how the church has suppressed the gospels that didn't fit the theology it wanted.

But this theory fails to take notice that nobody was dying for having a copy of the Gospel of Thomas. That's not true of the Gospel of Luke and Acts. If you were reading the book of Acts in the first century, then when you got to the part where Jesus ascended, I guarantee you would have glanced over your shoulder to make sure you were safe to read on. Because the ascension of Jesus meant something.

N. T. Wright explains, "From the pagan point of view, if the story [of the ascension] means anything, it means an implicit challenge to Caesar. The first thing we have to get our heads and hearts around as we read Acts is its unequivocal declaration and celebration of the fact that Jesus, the King of Israel, is the world's rightful Lord."[2]

Why Are You Just Standing Here?

I hope this book has helped you to see that Acts is so much more than a law book for church organization and worship rituals. It's a gripping account about men and women of faith who have taken risk after risk for the sake of something bigger than themselves.

As we approach the end of this book, I want you to remember the question that started all of this. Jesus has just ascended into heaven, and the angels appear and ask the disciples, "People of Galilee, why do you just stand here looking into the sky?"

What a strange question! It only makes sense in light of the ascension. Actually, the whole book of Acts only makes sense in light of the ascension. It is one reason the earliest Christians are seemingly unafraid of anything. The world's true Lord is back on the throne in charge of creation. All is as it should be in heaven.

This is why the angels ask the apostles, "Why are you just standing here? Jesus is the Lord of the universe, so get busy doing what he told you to do."

Time and time again in Luke's two volumes we find out that God is faithful to these people, even when his faithfulness means that they are going to lose their lives—especially when it means that they are going to lose their lives.

They still know the rightful king of the universe is back at the helm, so no petty ruler can stop them, no matter what he might use to scare them. Of course, this is not to say the rulers didn't try.

Court Dates

Before my last chapter's story of the shipwrecks and snakebites, Paul has been languishing in a prison cell for more than two years. He is waiting for his court date with a mid-level royalty guy named Felix. We know from history that this Felix is a real jerk.

Felix knows Paul came to town with a suitcase of money for the Jerusalem poor, so he thinks he can get Paul to offer him a bribe. But the joke is on Felix. He doesn't realize that Paul's main goal at the moment is to get to Rome. And he's perfectly happy to book this cruise on Rome's dime.

Felix never gets his bribe. He piddles with this for so long that he is replaced by another governor, a guy named Festus. Whose name makes him sound a lot happier than he actually is.

The Jewish leaders try another run at this whole let's-kill-Paul thing. They take Paul back to court under Festus and, while they are there, try to talk Festus into moving the venue for Paul's case back to Jerusalem.

To an unsuspecting foreigner like Festus, this request may sound reasonable, but it's actually like trying to hold a fair trial for a civil rights worker in the 1960s in Little Rock. Last time Paul was on trial in Jerusalem, the local leaders tried to assassinate him. Now, with a new governor in town, they are hoping for another shot at him. Their hope is that if Roman justice doesn't kill Paul, they can. And Paul knows what they have up their sleeve. So he appeals his case to be tried in Rome, by Caesar himself.

This is Paul's right as a Roman citizen. But it is not exactly the best move if he wants to stay alive. No one on this side of history thinks of Caesar as a compassionate person to plead to for mercy. But going to an unjust court in Rome certainly beats the alternative of returning to the lynch mob that awaits him in Jerusalem.

What no one realizes—not Festus, not Felix, nor the Jews, and maybe not even Paul—is how the hand of God manipulates this to accomplish his larger purposes. Paul appeals to Caesar in order to save his life, but it turns out to be the best thing he could have done for the spread of the gospel.

Once Paul does appeal to Caesar, the petty rulers have a problem. They have got to send this man to their boss, but they have no idea what to charge him with. He has not robbed any banks or cheated on his taxes or ripped off any old ladies. And none of them wants to send a prisoner, who just happens to be a Roman citizen, to Caesar's highest court without filing the paperwork that tells what crime he is being tried for.

Festus lucks out when a neighbor king, King Agrippa II, drops by for a state visit. Festus asks for advice from the more experienced ruler. And Agrippa is intrigued enough by Paul's bizarre life that he wants to meet him. So Festus sets up a court date just for Agrippa, but Agrippa doesn't come alone. He brings Bernice.

The names Agrippa and Bernice probably don't mean much to us today; but in that day, any mention of them would have been shocking. Because everyone knew who Bernice was.

Every generation has their envelope-pushing women (and men), but it seems we remember the women more. Madonna. Marilyn Monroe. Paris Hilton. And don't forget Bernice. Bernice may be the Miley Cyrus of her day. She is King Agrippa's sister, but they live together and travel together as man and wife. And people start talking.

The gossip gets so bad that eventually Bernice marries someone else. When that doesn't work out, she moves back in with Bubba. When Agrippa and his sister/lover arrive in Caesarea in Acts 25, everyone in town knows what kind of scandal is walking into that courtroom.

And the rumor mill worked just as well then as it does now. You'd go to the first-century grocery store and in the checkout lines the magazines would feature juicy stories like this one.

If by some slim chance you are reading this story for the first time, you have to be thinking, "These are the people who are going to judge a good man like Paul?" Going to court to get judged by people like this has got to feel like taking marriage advice from Donald Trump.

But this isn't going to stop Paul. He's got them right where he wants them. Because Paul doesn't want to talk about his case so much as he wants to tell his story—the one about him and Jesus. Once again Paul gets on his soapbox and preaches. And once again, they think Paul is crazy.

And they are pretty sure he'll probably be getting his last wish.

Nero the Nasty

The Caesar Paul is appealing to is a guy named Nero. He is a tyrant who makes Stalin look like Mary Poppins.

Nero first comes to power in the year A.D. 54, and he reigns for about fourteen years. No one really knows what to make of this Caesar at first. By all accounts, he is a flamboyant, artistic, and eventually violent man. He races chariots, he writes poetry, and he helps the Roman elite learn and appreciate good culture.

For example, to celebrate Nero's first shaving of his beard (which is a tradition I know we all look forward to), he has the noble elite of Rome take lessons in dancing and singing.

In his first days most people love him. He is bringing culture back to Rome. He is surprising and whimsical, and everything seems to be fine until there is a cataclysmic disaster. A massive fire broke out in the city of Rome. A large part of the city was destroyed. The fire devastated the city and crippled the Roman economy, not unlike the way the disasters of 9/11 hit the U.S. economy. Needless to say, the fire sank Nero's popularity level.

Nero, much like Adam and Eve, needed someone to blame.

He needed an easy target to make all the bad press go away, and he found his best option in this group of Christians that had already been confusing to the public. Nero decided to make them the bad guys.

He accused Christians of starting the fire, or at the very least, of causing the gods to be angry enough burn the city. Evidently, it worked. Christians, much like Jesus before them, became the focus of the wrath of the masses.

Nero, at his cruelest, even used some of these Christians as street lights, burning their tar-dipped bodies to light the night.

In his latter years, Nero became more and more paranoid. He began to kill people nearest to him, including his mother and step-brother. But the thing Nero will always be remembered for is his persecution of the Christians. He was the first Roman emperor who targeted Christians nationwide.

But the God who knows how to turn a cross into salvation for the world surely knows how to transform Nero's treachery into a victory for the gospel. What looked like a great disaster during Nero's most danger-ous days ended up being the greatest church growth strategy of all times.

Part of the problem with today's church is that we have bought into this idea that what it means to be the church involves only a small portion of our lives. A lot of us seem to think that we can believe the most radical things for one hour a week and then live just like everybody else. Such an assumption would have been unheard of for the first Christians.

In those days of severe persecution by Nero's goons, the gospel spreads and the church grows at an unprecedented pace. And Christians come out of this time of suffering more convinced than ever that, if the Lord is on their side, no one can beat them. Jesus' prediction turns out to be true: "The powers of death cannot prevail against my church."

If Jesus really is Lord, then what do you have to be afraid of?

Look at the last words of the book of Acts. Paul is a prisoner in Rome waiting to be tried by Nero, and this is when Acts fades to black. "For two whole years Paul stayed there in his own rented house and welcomed all who came to see him. Boldly and without hindrance he proclaimed the kingdom of God and taught about the Lord Jesus Christ" (Acts 28:30–31). For the past twelve chapters, Paul has been trying to get to Rome, to the capital of the world, to tell people that Jesus is Lord.

Now he's there, possibly on death row, waiting for his appeal to be heard by Nero, the craziest Caesar of them all.

This is the third in a row of back-to-back trial scenes, as if all of Acts is leading up to this moment. I know that most of us would really like to know how this story ends.

Does Paul live or does Nero kill him?

If you are asking if Paul died, however, you may be asking the wrong question, because Paul has reached a place in his faith where death can no longer touch him.

One reason Acts frustrates us so much is that we are asking, *How does this story end?* (does Paul die?) And Acts is asking, *Are you ready to live?*

Acts doesn't need to tell us what Caesar says because Caesar isn't Lord. Nero doesn't have the keys to life and death. He can't kill Paul. Nothing can, because Paul's life is hidden in Christ.

I think the reason we don't hear Caesar's judgment at the end of Luke's book could be that this is just another subtle way of saying what Acts has been saying all along.

That Caesar isn't Lord.

Getting in the Last Word

Do you know what the last word is in the book of Acts?

Unhindered.

Which is a surprising way to wrap this story up. I want to push back a little bit here. Hey, Luke, what do you call that prison guard Paul is chained to every day?

Unhindered? Have you checked out the weight of that chain on Paul's ankle, Luke? How would you like to wear steel handcuffs night and day?

Unhindered? You know better, Luke. At least you and Aristarchus can sneak off to Starbucks or go for a stroll along the Tiber. But Paul? He's on house arrest. For two years he's been homebound, and the calendar is still running when you put down your pen.

The amazing thing is that through all of this Paul never whines. He's been putting up with these hindrances for a long time when he tells us he has learned to be content—whatever.

Have we?

All of us have our share of hindrances.

If you don't have a chain on your leg like Paul, you may be hooked up to a school loan that looks like the national debt.

If you're not locked up with a Roman sentry, still you may be stuck at home with a disabled child or tied down by the constant needs of an aging parent.

Instead of "unhindered," some Bible scholars prefer to translate Luke's last word "unleashed." Now that's a word. It's pulsing with potential, just like the church it's trying to describe. Just think about what it means to be unleashed by God. Unleashed for the Kingdom of God, by the God of the Kingdom.

So your job would be a lot easier if you would trade in your integrity from time to time. Everybody else does it, and it would make it a lot easier to get ahead.

But you are unleashed from that, because Jesus is your Lord.

So you just graduated with your degree. And everyone around you in starting to climb a ladder that you could, too. You could build your own petty empire, but deep in your bones you feel as if God is calling you to serve "the least of these."

You can, because you are unleashed, because Jesus is your Lord.

So you're a parent, and your kids are starting to talk about taking this whole Jesus thing seriously, and maybe you realize just how dangerous these Bible stories are. Maybe you are thinking about trying to talk some common sense into them, but you know it would just be you passing on fear that they don't need.

You have been unleashed from fears like that. Not because bad things won't happen, but because Jesus is Lord.

Outlive Your Life

The word that comes right before "unleashed" at the end of Acts is "boldness." And that's a fitting image for the church. Because what do you do with a group of women and men who just aren't afraid of anything?

Paul's boldness, his willingness to do all he did, is one of the primary reasons that you and I know about the gospel today. For ten or eleven years, Paul travels through Europe and Turkey and Asia. He gets beaten, arrested, flogged, stoned, and shipwrecked. Then he would just dust himself off and move on. Because of this man's boldness, the story of Jesus got outside of Palestine and spread through the world.

So Luke's message in Acts isn't just some abstract history lesson for us. We stand on the shoulders of the boldness of men and women who sacrificed everything. If you are listening closely, you can hear their lives echoing a question to us.

Will you live as if this story is true?

The end of Acts is the beginning of our story. It's our job to take this story forward. Like Paul did.

Acts doesn't tell us what finally happened to Paul, but his last letters give us clues and tradition finishes the tale.

In the year 67, probably in the morning, his prison doors were opened. Guards quietly led him to an area of town that was reserved for beheading. And they did what Rome did so well. They put to death a man who has fought the entire second half of his life to tell people with his words and with his life the best story the world has ever known.

Paul's life ended that day; but in a very real sense, the influence of his life was just beginning.

The very next year, Nero, the guy who had all this seeming power and control, committed suicide for fear of being assassinated by his followers.

And today, people name their dogs Nero and their sons Paul.[3]

Because Caesar isn't Lord.

You know what life does? Life gives us plenty of opportunity to orient ourselves around the immediate, around the urgent.

Some kingdoms try to demand our immediate allegiance. But Luke is fighting to help us not do that. Did you know that Luke writes explicitly about the Kingdom of God almost forty times in his two books? And that's significant, because the Kingdom of God has never been just a good idea. In Judaism, it was always a political and a revolutionary concept.

That's why Luke's picture of the ascension matters. Look one more time at what N. T. Wright says:

> The claim that "Jesus is Lord" was never, in the first century, what we would call a religious claim pure and simple. There was no such thing as religion pure and simple. It was a claim about an ultimate reality which included politics, culture, commerce, family life and everything else you could think of. And if you stop saying "Jesus is Lord" out of deference to the private opinions of your friends and neighbours, Caesar smiles his grim smile and extends his empire by one more street. After all, the great eighteenth-century virtue of tolerance was developed not least by those who were keen on

extending their geographical or industrial empires, and who didn't want God breathing down their necks to stop them. Keep religion in the private sphere and we'll run the public square. And to that idea Luke says a clear No; and so must we.[4]

Rome made some pretty big claims. They said they were the hand of the gods, brought to bring the peace of Rome to the entire earth. They were a force that you didn't want to mess with. Nero at one point even made a statue to himself called the "Colossal Nero," because it was ninety-feet tall and made of bronze. But today, all that's left of it is just the pedestal it once stood on.

Paul's legacy is the people who gather to worship Jesus all around the world. They're everywhere. But I've been all over the Greco-Roman world, and you want to know the main legacy that Rome gave us? There are ruins everywhere.

These cities that once were so great, that once were testaments to the power of Rome, today are nothing but tourist bus stops.

But the Kingdom of God goes on.

This may sound like it's just a problem for the first century. But in every generation, in each of our lives, something competes for our worship, for our sense of security, or for our life. The Kingdom of God is the only safe bet.

Because if Jesus is Lord, that has to mean that Caesar or Felix or Festus isn't. And neither is our money, or our family, or our job.

This is the primary meaning of the ascension. That God is on his throne and there can be no other.

I wrote this book out of a hope that if we could just get a glimpse into what animated and motivated the earliest Christians, it would help us recapture some of what they had. It might help us imitate these raw, primal, wild people who turned the world upside down, not just for the sake of starting riots, but to set the world right.

The end of the book of Acts is our beginning.

Remember again how Acts started? "In my former book, Theophilus, I wrote about all that Jesus began to do and to teach" (Acts 1:1). Jesus began it, and it is our job to partner with the Spirit and keep it going.

In the church I serve we have talked about the book of Acts as a pattern. I want us to re-consider what that pattern really is. Alan Hirsch and Michael Frost say it this way:

> The early church was founded upon the images of Paul and his compatriots trekking mountain paths, taking beatings, enduring imprisonment and trials, contending with riots, surviving earthquakes, debating scholars and wizards, upsetting businessmen and religious leaders, as well as planting churches, preaching the gospel, and healing the sick. They formed the blueprint for the earliest models of Christian mission, models that presupposed risk, movement, energy, opposition, and triumph.[5]

Acts is indeed a pattern—a pattern for so much more than just what we do on Sunday mornings. It is a pattern for living exciting lives, unhindered by our greatest challenges, unleashed by God, for the glory of his Kingdom.

What God unleashed in the life, death, and resurrection of Jesus is available to God's people, the Body of Jesus.

So why are we just standing around?

We are unleashed.

Endnotes

Chapter 1

[1] Annie Dillard, *Teaching a Stone to Talk* (New York: Harper Collins, 2009), 52.

[2] http://www.relevantmagazine.com/issue-65-septoctober-2013.

[3] For more on this, see the book *unChristian* by David Kinnaman and Gabe Lyons (Grand Rapids: Baker Books, 2007).

[4] Genesis 4:23–24.

[5] Skye Jethani, *Futureville: Discover Your Purpose for Today by Reimagining Tomorrow* (Nashville: Thomas Nelson, 2014), 158.

[6] N. T. Wright, *Surprised by Hope* (New York: HarperOne, 2008), 50.

[7] Tom Wright, *Acts for Everyone* Part 1 (Westminster: John Knox Press, 2007), 46.

[8] Jethani, *Futureville*, 149–150.

[9] Barbara Brown Taylor, *Gospel Medicine* (Lanham, MD: Cowley Publications, 1992), 167.

Chapter 2

[1] Genesis 1:27.

[2] Isaiah 49:6.

[3] N. T. Wright, *Resurrection of the Son of God* (Minneapolis: Fortress, 2004), 652.

[4] Jean Vanier, *Community and Growth* (Mahwah, NJ: Paulist Press, 1989), 57.

Chapter 3

[1] Andy Crouch, *Culture Making* (Downers Grove, IL: InterVarsity Press, 2008), 154.

[2] Francis Spufford makes this point much more poetically in his book *Unapologetic: Why, Despite Everything, Christianity Can Still Make Surprising Emotional Sense* (London: Faber and Faber, 2014), 37.

Chapter 4

[1] Gray 2009 Toyota Tundra

[2] 1 Kings 21:7–10.

[3] http://www.americanrhetoric.com/speeches/
mlkivebeentothemountaintop.htm.

[4] Tom Long at Lipscomb University Preaching Symposium, 2009.

Chapter 5

[1] Remember when Jesus appears to Saul in Acts 8, his charge against Saul is that his persecution of the church is also persecution of Jesus. God's solidarity and victory are continued precisely through Jesus' ascension!

Chapter 6

[1] Patrick Carr, "Johnny Cash's Freedom," *Country Music,* April 1979, 53.

[2] Quoted in Michael Frost and Alan Hirsch, *The Faith of Leap: Embracing a Theology of Risk, Adventure, and Courage* (Grand Rapids: Baker Books, 2011), 24.

Chapter 7

[1] Eugene H. Peterson, *The Jesus Way* (Grand Rapids: Eerdmans, 2007), 31.

[2] Skye Jethani, *With: Reimagining the Way You Relate to God* (Nashville: Thomas Nelson, 2011), 27.

[3] Christian Smith, *Soul Searching: The Religious and Spiritual Lives of American Teenagers* (Oxford: Oxford University Press, 2009).

[4] Skye Jethani, *The Divine Commodity: Discovering a Faith Beyond Consumer Christianity* (Grand Rapids: Zondervan, 2009), 108.

[5] Judith Levine, *Not Buying It* (New York: Atria Books, 2007), 27.

[6] Skye Jethani, *The Divine Commodity,* 85–86.

Chapter 8

[1] Jonathan Martin, *Prototype: What Happens When You Discover You're More Like Jesus Than You Think?* (Carol Stream, IL: Tyndale House, 2013), 93.

[2] Eugene H. Peterson, *Christ Plays in Ten Thousand Places* (Grand Rapids: Eerdmans, 2005), 136.

[3] Tim Keller, *Walking with God Though Pain and Suffering* (New York: Dutton Books, 2013), 121.

Chapter 9

[1] I'm in debt to Don Golden and Rob Bell's book, *Jesus Wants to Save Christians* (Grand Rapids: Zondervan, 2008), for reframing this story for me. Specifically chapter 4.

[2] I'm borrowing this phrase from the great book by Rob Bell and Don Golden that I cited earlier in this chapter.

Chapter 10

[1] Dallas Willard, *The Spirit of the Disciplines* (New York: HarperOne, 1990), 175.

[2] Scot McKnight, *The Jesus Creed* (Brewster, MA: Paraclete Press, 2004), 22.

[3] Eugene Peterson, *Working the Angles: The Shape of Pastoral Integrity* (Grand Rapids: Eerdmans, 1989), 44.

Chapter 11

[1] Miroslav Volf, *Exclusion and Embrace* (Nashville: Abingdon Press, 1996), 129.

[2] As quoted by Leonard Sweet in *Nudge: Awakening Each Other to the God Who Is Already There* (Chicago: David C. Cook, 2010), 174.

[3] In Rob Bell's first book (one that didn't start a Twitter war), he makes a great point about this passage in connection with Jesus' observation that whatever his church "bound or loosed on earth, would be bound or loosed in Heaven." *Velvet Elvis* (Grand Rapids: Zondervan, 2006), 56–59.

[4] Acts 15:36–41.

[5] Michael Frost and Alan Hirsch, *ReJesus: A Wild Messiah for a Missional Church* (Peabody, MA: Hendrickson Publishers, 2008), 1–2.

[6] Timothy Keller, *Generous Justice: How God's Grace Makes Us Just* (New York: Dutton Books, 2010), 179–180.

Chapter 12

[1] Andrew Root, *The Promise of Despair: The Way of the Cross as the Way of the Church* (Nashville: Abingdon, 2010), 143.

[2] As quoted in Timothy Keller, *King's Cross* (New York: Penguin Books, 2011), 123–124.

[3] Erwin McManus, *The Barbarian Way: Unleash the Untamed Faith Within* (Nashville: Thomas Nelson, 2005), 48.

Chapter 13

[1] Michael Frost and Alan Hirsch, *The Faith of Leap: Embracing a Theology of Risk, Adventure, and Courage* (Grand Rapids: Zondervan, 2011), 104.

[2] Job 38:8–11.

[3] Rodney Stark, *The Rise of Christianity: How the Obscure, Marginal Jesus Movement Became the Dominant Religious Force in the Western World in a Few Centuries* (New York: Harper Collins, 1997), 82.

[4] Andrew Root, *The Promise of Despair: The Way of the Cross as the Way of the Church*, 134.

Chapter 14

[1] Frederick Buechner, *Listening to Your Life: Daily Meditations with Frederick Buechner* (New York: HarperCollins, 2009), 289.

[2] N. T. Wright's sermon, "Shipwreck and Kingdom: Acts and the Anglican Communion," Nottingham, June 28, 2005. Available at www.ntwrightpage.com.

[3] I heard this brilliant sentence in a sermon by Andy Stanley describing the life of Paul.

[4] N. T. Wright, "Shipwreck and Kingdom."

[5] Frost and Hirsch, *The Faith of Leap*, 105.